The Birth of Writing

The Emergence of Man

The Birth of Writing

by Robert Claiborne
and the Editors
of TIME-LIFE Books

TIME-LIFE INTERNATIONAL
(Nederland) B.V.

The Author: ROBERT CLAIBORNE, author of an earlier volume in The Emergence of Man Series, *The First Americans*, has a long-standing interest in intellectual and technological achievements of both recent and ancient times. Formerly an editor of TIME-LIFE BOOKS, he also co-authored *Time*, a volume in the LIFE Library of Science.

The Consultant: ROBERT D. BIGGS, Professor of Assyriology at the Oriental Institute of the University of Chicago, is associate editor of the *Assyrian Dictionary*, as well as editor of the *Journal of Near Eastern Studies*. He has been a member of a number of archaeological expeditions in Iraq and is the author of a recently published volume dealing with archaic Sumerian texts, *Inscriptions from Tell Abu Salabikh*.

The Cover: Under the direction of a priest, a scribe seated on the floor of a temple storeroom in ancient Sumer, birthplace of writing, records an inventory of beer jars, grain and produce on a clay tablet. Temples, which were seats of learning as well as centres of worship, trained the most skilled scribes for service as priests, officials and teachers.

Contents

Introduction

Among all the revolutionary creations of man, writing ranks as the supreme intellectual achievement. It was invented not once but perhaps as many as six separate times, in places as distant from one another as China and Central America. Each effort began with simple pictures and plain strokes or dots—adequate for recording objects and numbers. But abstract formulations—such as "I shall", "please grant" and "go quickly"—called for something flexible enough to record speech itself.

A form of writing that began to mirror the workings of the human mind and heart first came into being late in the Fourth Millennium B.C. in Mesopotamia, the seminal Middle Eastern area that also gave birth to the earliest farms, cities and technology. The inventors of this writing were probably Sumerians; their script evolved into the system of wedge-shaped marks called cuneiform. Meanwhile, hieroglyphic writing—the combination of pictures and signs that remains one of the most exquisite and complex scripts ever devised—was being developed to meet the needs of Egypt's royalty and priesthood. But perhaps more than the Egyptians, the Sumerians spread their use of writing across the full spectrum of their lives; they used it not only for everyday book-keeping and commercial dealings but also for recording the texts that governed their religion and philosophy.

The climax of writing's developmental stage came near the end of the Second Millennium B.C. with the emergence of the Phoenician alphabet—precursor of the printed script of the book you are holding in your hands. By stages far less tentative than those that preceded it, the alphabet led to the complex uses of writing we know today, and inevitably to their technological offspring, from the printing press to the high-speed computer printout.

In 1963, while participating in an archaeological expedition at Tell Abu Salabikh in Iraq, I shared in the discovery of a hoard of hundreds of clay tablets. On these inscribed clay tablets had been written countless prayers, hymns and proverbs—providing new insights into the intelligence, creativity and way of life of men who lived almost 5,000 years ago. For the ability to read their words today, all of us are indebted to a corps of dedicated—and often intrepid—19th-century adventurers, who were originally drawn to the sites of the ancient scripts for a variety of reasons: perhaps merely the romantic fascination with arcane and exotic locales or the practical pursuit of business opportunities or—yes—the fascination with the human past that moves so many of us. Whatever their motives at the beginning, having found the ancient inscriptions, they proceeded with courage and perseverance to the often hazardous, often impossible tasks of copying them and puzzling them out. Their work and their achievements served to grip the imaginations of the scholars who built on the foundations of the explorers' initial successes.

Even today, however, the story of writing and its beginnings is far from completely told: ancient writing systems discovered in Crete and Mexico and Pakistan remain largely impenetrable. And the decipherment of important cuneiform records, such as those of the Sumerians, has not automatically revealed the meanings of others; for instance, the Elamite script used by early settlers in Iran has not yet yielded its secret.

We have then much still to learn. But there will be more archaeological finds; as they are unearthed, and as scholars—supported by all that we already know and by all the modern tools of technology—discover the missing keys, it is certain that we will continue to have exciting new insights into man's still largely mysterious past.

It is by his writings, uniquely, that we truly come to know him; that we can finally, after the passage of long millennia, see inside his mind.

Robert D. Biggs
The Oriental Institute of the
University of Chicago

Chapter One: The Miracle of Writing

The time is 1700 B.C. The place: a nameless town on the river Euphrates in southern Mesopotamia, the region now occupied by Iraq. In the marketplace sits a scribe. With one hand he holds a flattened lump of moist clay, in the other a pointed stylus trimmed from a reed. By his side is a merchant named Nanni, addressing a letter to Ea-nasir, a business associate in the distant city of Ur. Rocking back and forth on his heels, Nanni dictates to the scribe his grievances against his associate in a matter of some substandard copper ingots:

"You did not do what you promised me," he complains. "You put ingots that were not good before my messenger and said: 'If you want to take them, take them; if you don't want to take them, go away!'" He pauses to allow the scribe to impress on the clay the little groups of wedge-shaped marks that record his annoyance. "What do you take me for, that you treat somebody like me in such a fashion?" he continues. "I have sent as messengers gentlemen like ourselves to reclaim my money, but you have treated me with contempt by sending them back to me empty-handed several times."

Nanni goes on in this vein as the scribe takes down his angry words. At last Nanni concludes: "Take notice that from now on I will no longer accept any copper from you that is not of fine quality.

I shall henceforth select the ingots individually in my own yard, and I shall exercise my right of rejection because"—and he spits at the thought—"you have treated me with contempt."

The scribe, completing the letter, hands it to Nanni. And Nanni, telling the scribe that he can collect his fee—a measure of barley—at his convenience during business hours, steps over to his office, where he sets the letter on a shelf to dry. Tomorrow it will be turned over to a messenger who is travelling by riverboat to Ur, about 200 miles from the Persian Gulf. In a week or two it will reach its addressee —who may finally pay the money demanded of him or reply in the same indignant vein or perhaps ignore the whole matter, as he has evidently ignored prior demands. The letter itself will probably be placed in Ea-nasir's business archives; later, it will be thrown on a rubbish heap to be buried under the accumulating rubbish of centuries.

Nanni's letter to Ea-nasir was discovered in Ur during excavations carried out in the 1920s and '30s. It was written in cuneiform, an ancient form of writing named for the shape of its word signs (from the Latin *cuneus*, a wedge). It was a direct descendant of the earliest-known form of writing, the picture script probably invented in Mesopotamia by the Sumerian people about 3100 B.C. Battered and worn after more than 30 centuries, the wedge-shaped marks on Nanni's clay tablet were still legible in the 20th Century, when the letter reached the desk of A. Leo Oppenheim, Professor of Assyriology at the University of Chicago. The language spoken by Nanni to the scribe is a tongue that no living man has ever heard. Nonetheless, thanks to earlier scholars, Oppenheim could make sense of it. In 1967 his

After a battle, two Assyrian warriors greet each other, while a pair of scribes compile a record of the numbers slain. Using a brush and papyrus, the scribe in the foreground is writing in Aramaic, an alphabetic script used by the Assyrians in the late Eighth Century B.C., when this relief was carved. His bearded colleague is making notes on a clay or wax-covered tablet in traditional Assyrian cuneiform script —writing in wedge-shaped signs invented 2,400 years earlier.

translation, adapted in the passages at the beginning of the chapter, appeared in a book where the complaints of the indignant Nanni to the delinquent Ea-nasir can be read today.

The merchant Nanni can speak across a gulf of nearly 4,000 years because of one of man's most extraordinary inventions in all his long history—writing. Indeed, writing ranks with such revolutionary achievements as the taming of fire and the development of agriculture, for like both these achievements it changed the very nature of life. Writing enabled human beings to co-ordinate their activities with those of their fellows long leagues away. Writing made possible the construction of societies far larger and more complex than had ever been known: city-states, kingdoms and empires. The ability to write allowed men to evolve thoughts and perform calculations of an intricacy not otherwise attainable, and thereby opened the way to mathematics and science.

What is this civilized thing called writing? The early Chinese looked upon it as a sacred means of communing with divine spirits and royal ancestors. Aristotle defined writing as "symbols of spoken words". The 18th-century French philosopher Voltaire said, "Writing is the painting of the voice". Modern linguists define writing less poetically as a system of human communication by means of conventional, agreed-upon signs that represent language. The signs must be capable of being sent and received, and mutually understood, and they must correspond to spoken words.

Though writing developed not much more than 5,000 years ago—only yesterday in the long cal-

This stone tablet, shown actual size, is one of the oldest examples of pictographic writing. The achievement of an urban civilization that flourished in the Mesopotamian city of Kish about 5,300 years ago, the tablet is inscribed on both sides with simply drawn pictures. Except for a foot, a hand and two heads, however, few of the symbols are recognizable, and their meanings can only be surmised. Scholars believe the foot in the lower left rectangle could mean either "go" or "come"; the profiled heads at the top could signify "man" or "slave".

endar of man's vengeance—its roots, like those of so many other inventions, lie further back in the past. Man approached writing by lengthy stages: the development of speech; the invention of pictures; the need to reinforce memory by storing information; the realization that pictures could be used for that purpose; and finally, the difficult trial-and-error process of adapting pictures so that they represented the sounds of speech.

Like speech, of which it is an extension, writing requires the capacity to make mental leaps. All languages include a few representational, or imitative, words that literally sound like the ideas they convey —such as "cough", "buzz" and "whippoorwill" in English. But the number of things or actions that can be identified by sound is obviously very limited, so that the vocabularies of all languages, everywhere, are overwhelmingly composed of arbitrary sounds whose relationships to their meanings are purely a matter of convention. "Cat" sounds nothing like the animal it identifies; "walk" bears no resemblance to the sound of footsteps.

When did human speech embodying such arbitrary abstractions begin to develop? Prehistorians argue over the extent to which modern man's ancestors, such as the Neanderthals of 100,000 years ago and the still earlier *Homo erectus* of more than a million years ago, were capable of speech in the current sense. Most of them agree, however, that by 40,000 years ago *Homo sapiens* must have been physiologically equipped for speech and capable of performing the mental gymnastics that are involved in speech and even writing.

Perhaps not coincidentally, at about that same time, an antecedent of writing appeared: pictures.

What the cave paintings and drawings of early man meant, and why they were made, are another fertile source of dispute among prehistorians. But there seems no doubt that the cave artist who drew a mammoth, whatever his reasons, intended not only to communicate something—the idea of a mammoth —but to do so in a manner that transcended speech.

Perhaps the painter intended his picture as a record. Certainly the roots of writing grow from the need to store information—reinforcing memory—and to communicate it at a distance beyond the range of the voice. Such communication, whenever it first occurred, represented the first stage of protowriting —writing in the embryo.

When might protowriting have first emerged? In the early 1960s a science writer named Alexander Marshack undertook a search for the answer to that question. One day while leafing through a pile of research material, Marshack noticed a photograph of a bone dug up in central Africa at an archaeological site dating from around 6500 B.C.—more than 3,000 years before the appearance of writing. On it were a dozen or so groups of scratches, ranging from three to 21 in number. Clearly they had been made deliberately —and they did not look like decorations. But if not decorations, what were they?

The search for an answer led the writer to study the work of prehistorians and the dusty collections of half a dozen museums. He found that the African bone was by no means unique: hundreds of similar bones, engraved either with groups of lines or with groups of dots, had been made by peoples in many parts of the world at periods stretching over more than 20,000 years. The earliest, from France, were dated around 30,000 years ago—just about the time

A Gallery of Primitive Pictographs

All the writing systems ever devised have evolved from pictures—initially simple, linear drawings that represented familiar objects. Scholars call these first elements of graphic communication protowriting; although unable to communicate the spoken word, they were capable of transmitting ideas in the form of images, and of serving as an aid to memory. Though the first pictorial messages may have been drawn as early as 20,000 years ago, the technique has been used in modern times among primitive cultures in Africa, Australia and the Americas. On these pages are examples dating from the 17th to 19th centuries, showing how members of North American Indian tribes, using very different styles, communicated on three diverse subjects.

In 1883, at the behest of the U.S. Indian agent in Dakota Territory, the chief of the Oglala Sioux listed the members of his band in the profiles shown here. The Indians' names can be read from the signs above their heads (left to right): The-Bear-Spares-Him, Iron-Hawk (the colour blue means "iron"), Red-Horn-Bull, Charging-Hawk, Wears-the-Feather and Red-Crow. The red streaks across the faces of the Indians indicate that they are warriors, the equivalent in rank of captains.

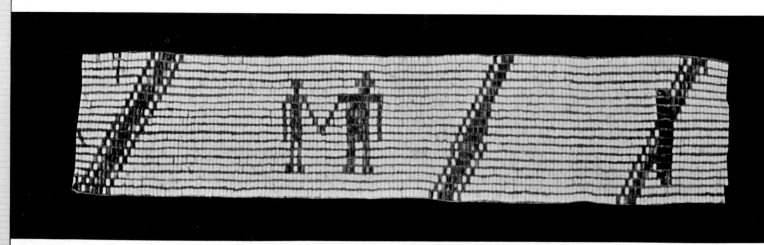

Two wampum-bead figures clasping hands—one in a white man's hat—record the Delaware Indians' treaty with William Penn.

Resembling childish renditions of wheels and stars, these drawings in ochre and brown are Indian rock paintings found in 1884 outside Santa Barbara, California, near an old Indian trail. Noting a similarity in their colours to those of 18th-Century Mexican blankets, some archaeologists suggest that the circles in the paintings represent bundles of blankets secured by cords (the crisscross markings). Since blankets were traded by the Indians to the priests of the Santa Barbara Mission, the pictographs could represent records of a trading expedition. The figure that appears to be a man could be the leader, wearing one of the striped blankets of the period.

that Cro-Magnon, the first truly modern man, appeared in that part of the world.

Putting the bones under a microscope, Marshack found subtle but consistent differences in the forms of the markings on any single bone. It seemed that each bone had been inscribed by means of various stone points with slightly different shapes. A line of 50 grooves on a bone might begin with five made with one tool, followed by a dozen made with a second tool, seven with a third and so on. The pattern of differently formed markings strongly suggested that they had been made over a span of time.

Marshack then began counting the markings on a number of bones. He decided that they often seemed to correspond, in both number and arrangement, to days in the cycle of the moon; the subgroupings of variant marks appeared to tick off the lunar phases —new moon, half-moon and full moon.

Not all prehistorians accept Marshack's theory that the marks are lunar notations, though many consider it plausible. Certainly the marks might equally well be tallies of reindeer speared in a series of hunts, or score sheets for some pastime whose rules have vanished with its players. What seems virtually certain, however, is that they represent tallies of something —whether days, reindeer or other things.

Whatever the subject may have been, it now seems probable that as early as 30,000 years ago men of the Old Stone Age, living in caves and clad in skins, had devised a system for storing information. This information probably would have been intelligible only to the person recording it in the first place—or perhaps to close friends and relatives. Even so, the markings on the bones represent what some specialists identify as the first stage of protowriting: the memory

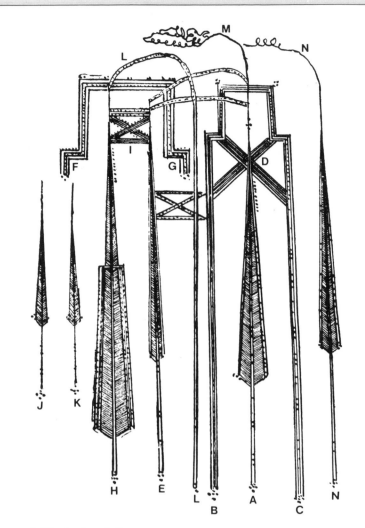

A Siberian love letter
Primitive techniques of pictorial writing—of the same type that led man to the earliest forms of true writing—have survived into modern times. This design is actually a letter from a young woman to a faithless former lover. It was composed early in this century by a girl of the Yukagir tribe, a group in northeast Siberia that today numbers some 600 members, few of whom still communicate this way.

The jilted girl's letter is remarkably poignant. It shows her (A) in skirt and pigtail (the dotted line near the skirt top), alone in her house (B-C), her plight represented by crossed bars (D) above her. Her former lover (E) lives at left (F-G), with a full-skirted, pig-tailed rival (H) who, the girl knows, now claims his affections. Though she recognizes their close bond, symbolized by the squared-in cross (I) above them, and predicts its fulfilment in the birth of two children (J and K), she feels the bitterness of separation, expressed by the heavy line (L) running from her rival's head down through the centre of the pictograph. Still, she perseveres in her passion, declared in the curlicue (M) floating above her head, though another (N) is in love with her.

aid, or mnemonic device, represented today by the proverbial string-around-the-finger.

Mnemonic devices of various sorts have existed throughout man's history. Among the commonest are notched tally sticks, which survived until recently in many parts of the world. In the early decades of this century some English and French farmers still used tally sticks to record the sizes of their harvests and the amounts of cash received. And only about a century and a half ago the august British Exchequer still kept records in the same form: according to one account, a fire that destroyed the Houses of Parliament in 1834 was set off by stoves that had become overheated while burning such out-of-date records.

Did the Cro-Magnon and other ancient peoples use tally sticks not just to record information but also to communicate it? Nobody knows, but it seems likely enough. Until recently, the Australian aborigines, whose material culture is rather like that of the Cro-Magnons, used tally sticks to send messages: two dozen notches could mean 24 men or women, or 24 objects, such as bags of red ochre; three notches might mean three days or three months.

Though the sticks conveyed information, these protowritings were essentially only memory aids. The real substance of the message was carried not by a stick but by its bearer, who would tell the recipient what was wanted—whether men, women or bags of ochre—and for what purpose; whether days or months were involved, and what was supposed to happen at the end of that time. The sticks served merely to remind the bearer of the numbers—and sometimes also to establish his credentials as an authentic representative of his tribal elder.

A more versatile type of memory aid is represented by the knotted cord, which not only is lighter than a tally stick but also can be corrected; knots, unlike notches, can be erased by untying. Legends of China say that the knotted cord was used to keep records in that land for centuries before writing was invented. As for the Western world, the Greek historian Herodotus describes how the great Persian king Darius, during an expedition against some troublesome Scythian horsemen, left a force of his Greek allies to guard a strategic bridge at his rear. On departing, he gave them a thong with 60 knots in it, ordering them to "loose one knot each day. If the days marked by the knots have all passed and I have not returned, take ship for your own homes." Darius meant that within 60 days he would either have returned safely —as he did—or suffered defeat and death.

Both the notch and knot forms of protowriting seem to have dealt primarily with numbers, not with the nature of objects in terms of such characteristics as shape, relative size, or sex. To record that kind of information about objects—as distinct from their numbers—the obvious method is to draw a picture. Sequences of pictures are known to have figured in the early stages of all true writing systems, and the same technique probably emerged even earlier as a variety of protowriting.

Some prehistorians have seen a possible early example of pictorial protowriting in the "coloured pebbles" of the Azilian culture, which flourished in southern France some 10,000 years ago; but the weight of scholarly opinion is that this theory almost certainly is incorrect. It is true that the Azilian designs—circles, stripes, crosses and the like painted on small stones—sometimes resemble symbols used in writing systems of later times. But they bear no resemblance whatever to the literal pictures that invariably form the earliest writing symbols. The Azilian pebbles, moreover, typically have only single signs painted on them; they lack the sequencing that is essential to qualify them as protowriting.

When pictures qualify, they are more useful than such other kinds of protowriting as the notched stick because they can serve as more than devices that merely jog the memory to recall a message already known; pictures can also convey a message to someone who has never heard it, without the agency of a human messenger. American Indians of many tribes used pictures as notices to friends and neighbours of where they had gone, or expected to go, and why. An Abnaki hunter in Maine, for example, might leave outside his wigwam a wikhegan, a scroll of birch-bark with a series of pictures: a man in a canoe and a deer; a man on foot pointing at a squiggle; a man on snow-shoes pulling a sled. The message is: "I am going across the lake to hunt deer; will turn off before reaching next lake; will be gone all winter."

Yet such varieties of protowriting, while they can convey ideas, do not record the spoken word. True writing begins when pictures, by their nature and by the sequence in which they are placed, are able to substitute for the spoken words of a given language.

In its very earliest stages writing could deal only with words that could be pictured—concrete objects and actions. A picture of a human head meant "head", a tuft of grain meant "barley". Quite early, however, the potentialities of this limited system were expanded in several ways. First, a picture of an object could be used as a sort of metaphor to suggest an object or concept that could not easily be pictured. Thus in Sumerian writing the sign for "mouth" also came to mean "speak".

A second way of extending the range of writing, used first by the Sumerians and today by the modern Chinese, was to combine two signs to form a third with a different meaning. In Sumerian the combined signs for "mountain" and "woman" expressed not "mountain woman" but "slave girl"—perhaps because the Sumerians obtained their slaves mainly from the mountain regions that lay to the north of their homeland. Similarly, the signs for "mouth" and "food" were combined to mean "eat". In Chinese the symbol for mouth combined with the symbol for door means "to inquire".

The key step in the development of writing came when a picture was used to represent not a given object but simply the sound of its name. This stage is called rebus writing, after the modern puzzles called rebuses: two pictures—say, one of an eye and one of a saw—symbolize the phrase "I saw". Through this system of visual punning, literal pictorial signs became converted into purely phonetic signs. The Sumerian sign for the word "water"—a in ancient Mesopotamia—began about 3100 B.C. as two wavy lines suggesting a rippling stream. By 2500 B.C., after evolving through stages into full-fledged cuneiform, the writing of the original symbol had been transformed into a sign made by three jabs of the stylus; the lines had straightened; the ripples had disappeared; and the sign no longer looked like water at all. But as the sign became simpler in appearance, it grew more complex in function. For it happened that in the spoken Sumerian language the word a meant the preposition "in" as well as the noun "water"; and now, the one sign was able to do double duty. What

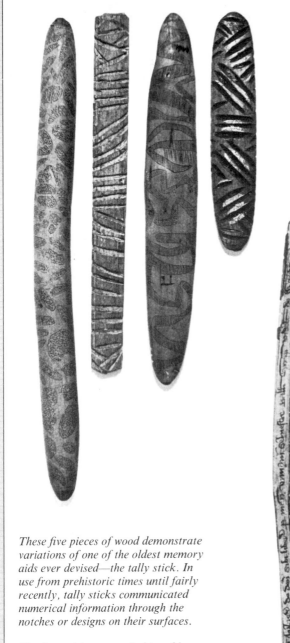

These five pieces of wood demonstrate variations of one of the oldest memory aids ever devised—the tally stick. In use from prehistoric times until fairly recently, tally sticks communicated numerical information through the notches or designs on their surfaces.

The four sticks at top, fashioned by Australian aborigines, bear a curious assortment of designs ranging from pinpoints cut in the wood (left) to incised bars (right). Such primitive sticks required a human messenger to interpret for the recipient the kinds of objects or people that the tally sticks enumerated. Less primitive is the example at right of a type used by the British Exchequer to record receipts from about 1100 to 1826. Such sticks usually bore some explanatory notes.

had taken place was a shift from pictorial writing to phonetic writing.

That shift transformed writing into the basic tool of civilization. For the early societies that first devised writing, the new tool meant that human activities could be organized systematically. Merchants and craftsmen, instead of relying on miscellaneous goods brought their way by random trade, could order in writing precisely what they wanted, with some assurance that they would get it—though not necessarily without disputes like that between Nanni and Ea-nasir. The written IOU gave the lender a claim on the borrower that would survive the death of either. The written deed ensured that the landholder could retain control of his acres through all but the most extreme social disorders. Temple priests could keep written inventories of offerings from the pious and pass them on to their sacerdotal successors, thereby ensuring their own good repute with the gods —and the continued prosperity of the priesthood.

Writing was influenced by kings no less than it was by priests. The unification of Egypt about 3100 B.C. into a kingdom that stretched a thousand miles along the Nile probably hastened the development of the first Egyptian hieroglyphic writing, which occurred around that time. Similarly, in Mesopotamia the development and spread of cuneiform ties in with the growth of city-states, kingdoms and empires.

To govern a large community or a distant colony means above all to communicate with its members: to order, forbid and give guarantees. Of course, instructions and promises can be transmitted by word of mouth, but verbal injunctions are easily garbled or forgotten or lost; and these difficulties multiplied as city-states expanded into kingdoms.

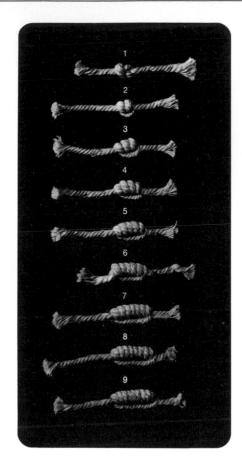

After more than 500 years, the knots in the quipu at the right are too worn to be read. But to indicate the principles on which the device was based, simple numbers have been reconstructed in the key above, and the quipu itself has been spread out, though it rarely was in actual use; ordinarily the cords hung down like the strands of a mop.

The knot represented values in a decimal system, and the absence of a knot denoted zero. But values varied according to the knot's specific position on the cord and the type of knot used. The cords, in turn, were tied off in bunches by additional strands, called summation cords (stretching up in the picture at right). The knots on the summation cords provided the total value of each bunch of pendant cords.

Many-tasselled Strings to Keep Accounts

Arriving in South America in the 16th Century, the Spanish conquistadors encountered the empire of the Incas, a vast realm that flourished without benefit of the wheel or the draught animal. The empire was also the world's only society ever to maintain an advanced level of civilization without knowledge of the written word.

One explanation for the success of the Incas—despite their ignorance of writing—was their ability to keep meticulous records by means of a device using an intricate system of knotted cords. Called a quipu—an Indian word meaning knot—the device consisted of a principal cord from which hung many bunches of pendant cords (*near left*). Each bunch might represent a different subject being tallied. The hanging cords were tied at specific intervals with various types of knots, each representing a different numerical value (*samples, far left*). For example, a string with two overhand knots above a group of four overhand knots surmounting a five-fold-long knot meant "245".

Each Inca-ruled town and village had a hierarchy of *quipucamayocs*, or knot keepers, whose job was to tie and interpret the knot records. Thus even in the absence of a writing system, the Incas were able to control an empire that, at its zenith, spread over more than 300,000 square miles. The quipus permitted authorities to maintain an up-to-date census, to organize the population into administrative units of as few as 10 families and to assess taxes, paid in the form of labour.

So well, in fact, did the empire function under the quipu system that for a while before the Spaniards completed their conquest, they allowed the routine of government to continue as before—eloquent testimony to the efficiency of the knotted cords.

Important and useful as writing was as a practical tool of commerce and administration, it was also a way of reinforcing a people's spiritual commitment. To spoken words, which may have their own incantatory power, writing added the special dimension of permanence; a blessing or curse set down in written symbols seemed to be invoked perpetually. Towards that end the Egyptian pharaohs and nobles more than 4,500 years ago inscribed their tombs with formulas to ensure that their afterlife would be spent in the sky with the gods, including Re, the sun, and Thoth, the moon. On the tomb of one notable are the words: "You that voyage over the sky, Re and Thoth, take him unto you to be with you, that he may eat of that whereof you eat; that he may drink of that whereof you drink; that he may live on that whereon you live; that he may dwell there where you dwell; that he may be strong wherein you are strong; that he may voyage there where you voyage." A hopeful inscription on the tomb of another pharaoh says, "He rushes at the sky like a heron, he has kissed the sky like a hawk, he has leapt skywards like a grasshopper."

The tombs also bear curses against the enemies of the departed, expressed as if they had already happened: "Poverty has taken their inheritances, their dwellings, a high Nile their gates." Later inscriptions invoke special imprecations on those who would disturb the dead man's remains, or rob his tomb.

Of all the many consequences of writing, perhaps none is more significant than its contribution to man's understanding of himself and of the universe in which he lives. Recorded history begins with the birth of writing; in most societies, so do science and philosophic thought. Writing allows the reader to conjure up the human past and permits the student of man to reconstruct the life of his long-gone forbears in often startling detail: not merely what they looked like, but the food they ate and how they got it; how they sheltered and clothed themselves; and how they produced increasingly intricate artifacts to meet their physical and spiritual needs.

The mind of preliterate man can be fathomed only through the mute testimony of the artifacts dug up by the archaeologist's spade; but literate man speaks in his own voice. Four thousand years ago an Egyptian scribe fully understood the value of his profession: "A man has perished and his body has become earth," he wrote. "All his relatives have crumbled to dust. It is writing that makes him remembered."

Like many a tool—and many a talisman—writing was invented in many places, often independently. Over a period of more than 2,000 years—roughly from 3000 to 1000 B.C.—it arose in more than half a dozen societies, though several of the later inventions were not wholly original; some of the inventors apparently knew that writing existed among other peoples.

The social conditions that gave rise to writing are summed up in a historic phenomenon called the Urban Revolution: the growth of large and populous communities, which usually (though not invariably) congregated in cities. In these communities, the conditions of men became diversified and relationships among them grew complex. In the cultures of the Old Stone Age (800,000-9000 B.C.), everybody hunted and gathered food; in the first agricultural societies of the New Stone Age (9000-5000 B.C.), farmers and herdsmen joined the hunter-gatherers. The urban societies of a few thousand years later included not only farmers and herdsmen, but also craftsmen, merchants,

Writing—an Evolutionary Chronology

c.100,000-40,000 B.C.
Modern man evolves physiological capability of speech.

c.30,000 B.C.
Primitive cave paintings appear in Europe.

c.20,000-6500 B.C.
Notches on animal bones, a forerunner of writing in Africa and elsewhere, indicate beginnings of record keeping.

c. 3500-3000 B.C.
Earliest-known pictographic writing appears in Sumer.

c.3000 B.C.
Egyptians use hieroglyphic writing—a combination of pictures and symbols—on tombs, temples and monuments.

c.2800-2600 B.C.
The Sumerian writing system becomes cuneiform—lines of wedge-shaped signs reading from left to right.

c.2500 B.C.
Cuneiform begins to spread throughout the Middle East.

c.2300 B.C.
Indus Valley people use pictorial symbols on seals made for stamping and signing personal property.

c.2000 B.C.
Sequential pictographic inscriptions, considered a true system of writing, appear on seals and clay tablets in Crete.

c.1500 B.C.
Hittites invent their own form of hieroglyphic writing; Chinese develop ideographs—characters representing whole ideas—and carve them on bronze vessels and oracle bones.

c.1400 B.C.
People in the trading port of Ugarit devise an alphabet.

c.1100-900 B.C.
Phoenicians spread precursor of modern alphabet across the Mediterranean Sea to Greece.

c.800 B.C.
Greeks develop concept of modern alphabet, with vowels.

priests and eventually rich men and poor, freemen and slaves, debtors and creditors, taxpayers and tax collectors—and, of course, rulers and the ruled.

As the Urban Revolution gathered momentum in the Fourth Millennium of the pre-Christian era, the increasing complexity of the relationships among all these sorts and conditions of people, occupying ever-larger territories, created the social circumstances in which writing could take root. Men badly needed a means of reconciling conflicting claims between diverse groups, and techniques of recording and communicating agreements that would withstand the vagaries of human memory and the space limitations of the human voice. Writing, which came to fill these needs, was—like every other important invention—a product of its time.

The Sumerians, thought to be the first inventors of writing, inhabited southern Mesopotamia in the Fourth Millennium B.C. Their earliest script appears in the archaeological record around 3100 B.C., as the Urban Revolution was getting into stride. Soon afterwards, writing was reinvented nearly a thousand miles away by the Egyptians. It is likely enough that the Egyptians got the idea of writing from the Sumerians—there is archaeological evidence of contact between the two areas at this time—but the bare idea is all the Egyptians could have taken. For one thing, the Egyptian script is different in its symbols. The pictures used in the early stages of both systems vary, even when they were intended to portray the same object. The Egyptians, who invented the system of writing called hieroglyphs, portrayed the word "mouth" with a plain oval; the Sumerians, whose writing evolved into cuneiform, initially portrayed the mouth in a whiskered face.

The means of recording both systems were no less different. The Sumerians inscribed their pictures on soft clay tablets; the Egyptians carved theirs on stone monuments, or painted or drew on bits of pottery and, quite soon, on rolls of papyrus, a kind of paper made from the fibres of the papyrus plant that grew in abundance along the Nile.

Sometimes around 2500 B.C., writing was invented for the third time by the Elamites, whose territories lay in an area now occupied by Iran, about 200 miles east of Sumer. The Elamite script is puzzling to scholars, who have not yet succeeded in deciphering more than a few fragments. How the script came into existence and what course of development it followed also remain a puzzle. In any case, the inhabitants of Elam later discarded their own script and took over cuneiform, adapting the Sumerian signs to the phonetics of their own language.

In the same period, writing was invented yet again by the civilization centring in the Indus Valley, in present-day Pakistan. Here, as with Egypt and Elam, there is archaeological evidence of contact with Sumer. But once more the script is quite different; and so, it seems, are the implements of writing. The few surviving inscriptions were carved on stone seals and monuments, but everyday documents would obviously have called for more convenient materials. The people of the Indus Valley certainly did not use papyrus, which does not grow there, and almost as certainly not clay tablets, since not one has been unearthed by archaeologists. Presumably the people of the Indus wrote on something perishable, such as wood or leather, that has since rotted away.

Soon after 2000 B.C. writing was invented for the fifth time, in the maritime kingdom of Crete. The Cretans almost certainly got the notion of writing from foreign parts—probably from Egypt, with which they carried on regular trade—but the actual script is highly original. The Cretans, who began writing at some unknown date, were by the 17th Century B.C. employing two scripts, called Linear A and Linear B by modern scholars. As the names indicate, both were cursive scripts written in characters formed of lines, not of pictures. What relation A and B bear to each other has not been determined. Some experts believe that they developed simultaneously to serve different languages; some say that B arose out of A. All that has been settled in the wake of much scholarly disagreement is that Linear B was used for keeping palace inventories; Linear A may have been used for the same purpose, but no one can be sure.

Crete has also provided one of the strangest artifacts in the history of writing: the Phaistos disc (*page 127*), named for the palace where it was found. The symbols on the clay disc are totally unlike those of the linear scripts, which suggests that the disc may have been imported—though the possible source is just as obscure as the meaning of the disc's spirally arranged signs. One of the most striking features of the disc is the fact that its symbols were impressed with stamps instead of a stylus, the tool usually associated with writing on clay. This technique is regarded by some scholars as an astonishingly early anticipation of printing.

By 1500 B.C. another invention of writing had appeared in Asia Minor—a script called Hittite hieroglyphs, though the forms of the characters bear no resemblance to those of Egyptian hieroglyphs.

Hittite hieroglyphs were written in alternating directions, as an ox ploughs a field. The script numbered as many as 419 symbols, most of them pictographic. After decades of work that began in 1874, the script was finally deciphered in the 1960s—one of the great triumphs in the history of decipherment.

Interestingly, the Hittites used hieroglyphs when they set about carving inscriptions on stone monuments and rocks, many of them in far-flung Syrian outposts, but for everyday purposes they wrote in cuneiform, which they had borrowed from Mesopotamia and adapted to their own language.

At about the same time, writing was invented again, far to the east, in the valley of the river Yellow in China. That this invention was somehow triggered by contacts with the literate societies of western Asia is possible. But in view of the distance (4,500 miles across the Himalayas) between the two centres of civilization, the connection is unlikely; Chinese scholars reject the notion. Early Chinese symbols are pictorial and clearly indigenous, as are the writing materials: bamboo and silk. Modern Chinese, a direct descendant of this early script, is the oldest living writing with a continuous history.

From these beginnings many new scripts were to arise and further refinements were to be made. The revolutionary advance to alphabetic writing was to effect a quantum leap in the growth of writing. Scholars can now see that the process of development, from the earliest-known forms of writing to the latest, has been more or less continuous. But the 5,000-year span separating the birth of ancient writing from modern times posed a formidable problem for scholars and archaeologists. When in the 18th Century they began their attempts to decipher the inscriptions on Egyptian tombs and Mesopotamian tablets, they had to start virtually from scratch.

Uncovering the Mysteries of Imperial Egypt

Napoleon's invasion of Egypt in 1798, frustrated by British seapower, was a military fiasco. But because Bonaparte brought along scores of scholars and artists on the campaign, he was triumphant in opening the eyes of the world to the splendours of a forgotten civilization. Among other discoveries, the expedition found massive ruins covered with hieroglyphs—mysteries that seized the imagination of soldier and savant alike.

The artists devoted three years to drawing the remains and copying the strange characters carved or painted on them. Starting in 1809, the results were published in the 19-volume *Description de l'Egypte* (source of the pictures on these pages), further stimulating interest in that ancient land and in the story hidden behind its baffling inscriptions.

The key to the story turned out to be the Rosetta stone (*page 40*), discovered by one of Napoleon's men; the stone was engraved not only in hieroglyphs but in Greek. Comparing the known language with the unknown one, the French scholar Jean-François Champollion set to work deciphering the hieroglyphs. It was in 1822 that Champollion succeeded, and Egypt's long silence was ended.

The shattered stone figure of Pharaoh Ramses III, rising from the rubble of the temple at Karnak, near Thebes, dwarfs one of Napoleon's artists.

Approaching the site of the ancient city of Thebes—a vast complex of ruins that included these obelisks, walls and columns of the Temple of Luxor—Napoleon's army was so impressed, according to one witness, that "it halted of itself, and, by one spontaneous impulse, grounded its arms". The artist, when sketching this view of the temple, included contemporary structures that partly obscured the pictures on the walls. The carved scenes celebrated an exploit of another formidable army: the charge of chariot-borne archers under Pharaoh Ramses II against the Hittites in 1300 B.C.

Though many of Egypt's ruins had become neglected relics even in antiquity, these figures towering above the desert near Thebes—the Colossi of Memnon, remnants of a vanished temple—continued to lure curious visitors through Greek and Roman times. After an earthquake cracked the right-hand statue in A.D. 27, its sun-warmed stone emitted sounds in the early morning, which ancient witnesses interpreted as a god's voice. But the eerie noises had long ended by the time a French artist drew reconstructions of the figure from two perspectives (opposite) during the late 1700s. The drawings incorporate not only Egyptian hieroglyphs but also later writings carved on the original by Greek and Roman visitors.

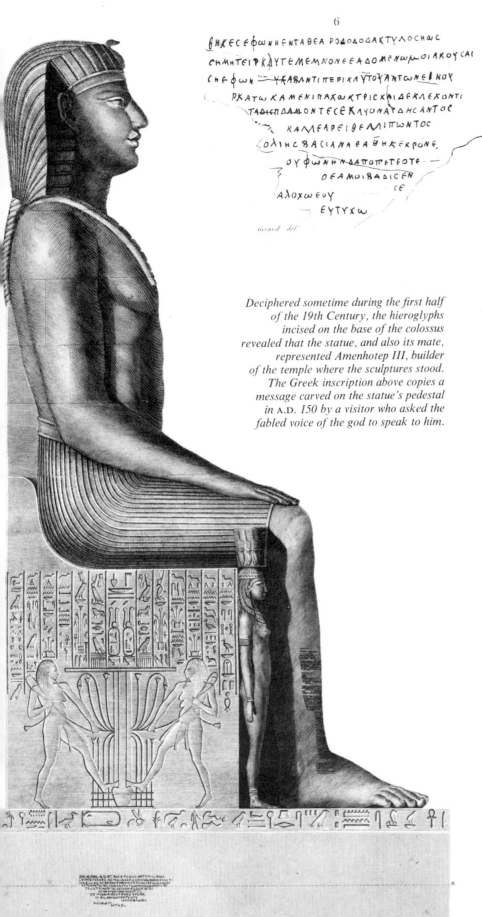

ΘΗΚΕΣΕΦΩΝΗΕΝΤΑΘΕΑ ΡΟΔΟΔΟΔΑΚΤΥΛΟΣΗΩΣ
ΣΗΜΗΤΕΙΡΚΛΥΤΕΜΕΜΝΟΝΕΕΑΔΟΜΕΝΗΩΜΟΙΑΚΟΥΣΑΙ
ΣΗΕΦΩΝΗ ΥΚΑΒΑΝΤΙΠΕΡΙΚΛΥΤΟΥΑΝΤΩΝΕΙΝΟΥ
ΡΚΑΤΩ ΚΑΜΕΝΙΠΑΧΩΚΤΡΙΣΚΑΙΔΕΚΛΕΧΟΝΤΙ
ΤΑΔΗΠΠΔΑΜΟΝΤΕΣΕΚΛΥΟΝΑΓΔΗΣΑΝΤΟΣ
ΚΑΜΓΑΡΕΙΘΕΛΠΤΩΝΤΟΣ
ΟΛΙΗΣΒΑΣΙΑΝΑΕΑΘΗΚΕΚΡΟΝΕ.
ΟΥΦΩΝΗΝΔΑΠΟΤΡΤΕΟΤΕ
ΘΕΑΜΟΙΒΑΔΙΣΕΝ ΣΕ
ΛΟΧΩΕΟΥ
ΕΥΤΥΧΩ

Girard del

Deciphered sometime during the first half
of the 19th Century, the hieroglyphs
incised on the base of the colossus
revealed that the statue, and also its mate,
represented Amenhotep III, builder
of the temple where the sculptures stood.
The Greek inscription above copies a
message carved on the statue's pedestal
in A.D. 150 by a visitor who asked the
fabled voice of the god to speak to him.

The full significance of this lively bas-relief, copied from a temple at Medinet Habu for inclusion in Description de l'Egypte, remained obscure until scholars learned to read the inscriptions surrounding the human figures. Prisoners were apparently being offered to the chariot-borne figure of the high-ranking Egyptian at right, but his identity and the occasion were puzzling. Once understood, the hieroglyphs disclosed that the relief—one of some 40 on the temple walls illustrating the 12th Century B.C. military achievements of Ramses III—showed the Pharaoh celebrating a victory over the Libyans. As the captives are presented to the ruler, scribes tally the severed hands of those slain in the battle.

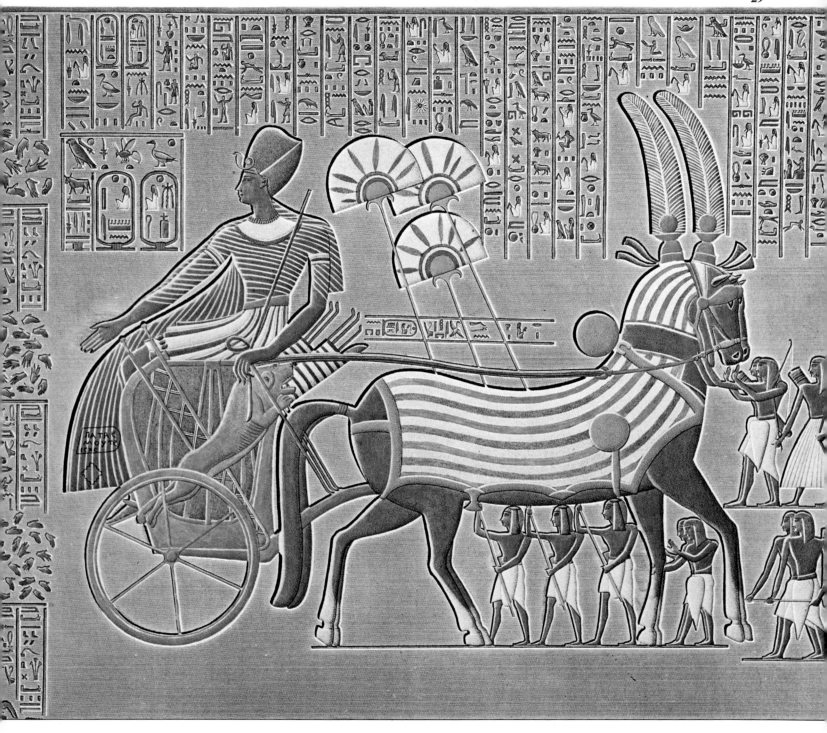

This meticulously rendered view of the portico of Isis' temple at Philae, as it might have looked when in use, helped fire the enthusiasm of 19t.

entury Europeans to delve deeply into the lore of ancient Egypt. The inscriptions on the columns and walls describe royal gifts to the gods.

Most persons, if asked to decipher a message in an unknown language and an unknown script, would not have the remotest notion of how to begin. In the history of decipherment, two ways of relating the known to the unknown have been of fundamental importance. The easier method works through a bilingual inscription: a message expressed in two different languages written side by side. The other, much more difficult, relies on linguistic correspondence, a scholar's phrase reflecting the fact that languages come in families, with definable similarities.

If one of the languages in a bilingual inscription can already be read and understood, the decipherer has a translation before him, and from that can get the gist of the unknown message. But even if he is fortunate enough to possess a bilingual text, the task is extremely complicated, because languages do not bear symmetrical resemblances to one another, and neither the logic nor the structure of the one language will necessarily follow the logic or the structure of the other, word for word or even phrase for phrase.

All the same, a bilingual text offers a much more direct route to solving an unknown tongue than does the alternative—linguistic correspondence. This latter method, though complex, arises from a simple premise: very few languages stand alone; most of them are related, closely or distantly, to other languages. English, for example, is closely related to the Teutonic languages—German, Dutch and the Scan-

dinavian tongues. French, a Latin language, is related to Italian, Spanish and Portuguese. Both groups —along with Greek, Russian and some of the tongues in the Indian subcontinent—belong to a large family of Indo-European languages that bear resemblances to one another but stand apart from Hebrew and Arabic (of the Semitic family) and Chinese and Burmese (of the Sino-Tibetan family).

This principle was unknown when the rise of science, a relish for commerce and a general urge for exploration combined to awaken European interest in the East beginning in the early 17th Century. The idea of linguistic correspondence came to light largely through the insight of an English jurist named William Jones, who in the 1780s was stationed in India as an officer with the British East India Company—a creation of the British Parliament designed to give England a monopoly on Eastern trade. Jones set about studying Sanskrit, an ancient Indian language, in order to comprehend some old local legal codes written in the Sanskrit tongue.

Already fluent in Greek and Latin, Jones began to realize that Sanskrit had some striking affinities with European languages. The Sanskrit word for "snake", *sarpa*, resembled the Latin *serpens* (from which the English "serpent" is derived); the Sanskrit word *pra* came close to the Greek and Latin *pro*, meaning "for", and the Sanskrit word *ped* (foot) suggested *pes* in Latin and *pous* in Greek. From these and many other correspondences, Jones concluded that the resemblances between Sanskrit, Greek and Latin were so strong "that no philologer could examine all three without believing them to have sprung from some common source which, perhaps, no longer exists".

The common source that Jones suspected had, in

Holding on his lap a partially opened roll of papyrus—a symbol of his revered profession—an Egyptian scribe named Kay sits in the customary cross-legged scribal posture. Excavated at Sakkarah in the 19th Century, the 4,500-year-old limestone statue has some original paint still clinging to it. The eyes are inlaid with white quartz, crystal and ebony.

fact, existed. It is now known as Indo-European, a language that scholars conjecture may have been spoken some time before 4000 B.C. in eastern Europe, perhaps somewhere in the Danube valley. From this source eventually came Sanskrit (and thence virtually all the modern languages of Pakistan and India) and Persian; and in the West, Greek, Latin and nearly all the European languages.

From the linguist's point of view, the important fact governing similarities and differences between related languages is their general consistency—which results in predictability. An English-speaking student beginning to study German, once he learns that *haus* means "house", will not be much surprised to learn that *maus* means "mouse"; in both cases the German "au" corresponds to the English "ou"; other examples of correspondence occur in both languages.

The same principle operates in favour of a scholar trying to decipher a strange script. If he can establish that the unknown language he is trying to read is related to a known language, he can then obtain clues to the meaning of many words by establishing correspondences of the "au-ou" type.

When early 19th-century scholars first began attempting to unravel the secrets of ancient scripts, these principles of decipherment—comparison of bilingual texts and linguistic correspondence—existed in theory, but they were far from being tools lying ready to the decipherer's hand; a wall of ignorance separated the ancient world from the modern. Such was the case with Egyptian, the first ancient script to attract the attention of modern European scholars. In the 18th Century little was known about Egypt's past, though surviving accounts in Greek and Roman writings and in the Bible clearly showed that the Egyptians had once possessed a mighty civilization. The pyramids, which ranked among the Seven Wonders of the World, still stood on the banks of the Nile to astonish European travellers.

Obviously the Egyptians had been a literate people: carved and painted inside some of the pyramids and temples were elaborate little pictures that Herodotus and other classical authors had described as writing. But no man could read the pictures—not even native Egyptians. In the 17th Century A.D. most Egyptians spoke the Arabic tongue imposed on them by Muslim conquerors a thousand years earlier, and they wrote in the elegant swirls of the Arabic script. A dwindling minority spoke Coptic, which survived as the sacred language of the Coptic Christian Church and was written in a variation of the Greek alphabet.

Of the classical authors who mentioned Egyptian writing, only one discussed the subject extensively—and he, as later research has established, was unreliable. The writer was Horapollo of Nilopolis (Nile City). Writing in Coptic around A.D. 300, Horapollo made an effort to decipher the Egyptian hieroglyphs. By the 17th Century his books had been translated into Greek, unluckily for subsequent generations of scholars. His account mingled a bit of fact with much fiction—and some outright fantasy.

Horapollo stated, correctly, that the hieroglyphic picture of a vulture signified "mother"—but he built his logic on an absurd premise: that only female vultures existed in nature. (The actual connection, as it happens, rests on the fact that the spoken words for "mother" and "vulture" had similar sounds in Egyptian.) In a flight of sheer fancy, Horapollo went on to claim that a picture of the front paws of a lion meant

Early hieroglyphs identify the figures on an Egyptian commemorative plaque of about 3100 B.C., marking a victory of King Narmer (centre) over his enemies. Framed in a rectangle above Narmer is his name, written with the signs of a fish and a chisel, representing syllables that approximate nar and mer. The undeciphered names of his retainer (left) and his humbled adversaries (lower right and bottom) are carved near their heads. The story of Narmer's triumph is retold at top right: a falcon, symbol of the conquering king, treads on papyrus plants that represent the subjugated region, while leading the defeated enemy by the nose.

"strength" because "they represent the beast's most powerful limbs". He compounded such mistakes by supposing that every sign stood for an entire word, and by concluding that all the writings dealt with abstruse mystical and philosophical concepts that were intelligible only to priests.

The first learned men of the modern era did little better than Horapollo, though one of them, a German Jesuit and professor of mathematics named Athanasius Kircher, was to make a vital contribution to the work of later scholars. In 1628, soon after being ordained, Kircher accidentally ran across some engravings of hieroglyphs in a library and promptly plunged into an attempt to translate them.

In this he failed. For example, he translated one group of seven signs as "The life of things, after the victory over Typhon, the humidity of nature, through the vigilance of Anubis". It would be hard to say what this interpretation meant even to Kircher, though he was undoubtedly influenced by Horapollo's notion that the language was a deliberately mysterious priestly jargon. (The true meaning of the group of signs is simple: "Osiris says".)

Still, it is easy to see why Kircher fell into a trap. The phrase contained seven symbols, and because each one looked like a picture of something, Kircher assumed, as others would long continue to do, that each one stood for an idea. That the pictures corresponded to some of the sounds in the ancient Egyptian language did not occur to Kircher any more than it had to Horapollo.

In other endeavours, however, Kircher was more successful. He was a well-grounded scholar, and he studied Coptic as well as hieroglyphs. He eventually compiled and published a Coptic-Latin dictionary

A Revived Passion for Old Monuments

After Napoleon's expedition opened the world's eyes to the glories of ancient Egypt (*pages 23-31*), interest in archaic styles was galvanized, influencing both architecture and design for the following century.

Europe could not contain its passion for obelisks, pylons, cornices, columns and floral capitals; their exotic appeal soon travelled across the Atlantic to the United States to dominate such constructions as the Washington Monument—which at 555 feet is far taller than any Egyptian obelisk —the Bunker Hill Monument (*right*), churches, burial vaults, railway stations and even prisons (*opposite, top*).

In 1881 the trend culminated in the importation of an authentic Egyptian obelisk (*opposite, bottom*); donated by the Egyptian government, the monument was shipped 5,000 miles across the sea to be erected in New York City's Central Park.

Rising 221 feet above Charlestown, Massachusetts, the Bunker Hill Monument commemorates Americans who died fighting the British in 1775. Shown in a 19th Century print, the monument was dedicated in 1825 by Daniel Webster as part of the cornerstone-laying ceremonies. Completed 18 years later, the structure had an interior staircase leading to windows at the top, a feature never incorporated in Egyptian obelisks.

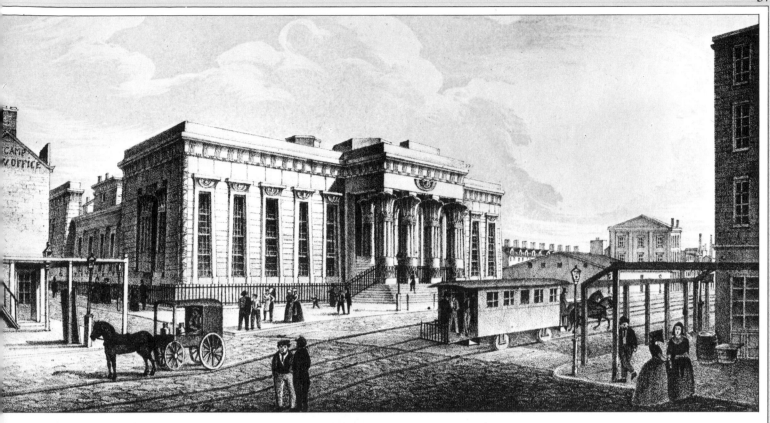

In 1838 New Yorkers built this ponderous edifice in lower Manhattan to serve as both a court house and prison. First of several New York gaols called the "Tombs", the building was dismissed by the visiting English writer Charles Dickens as a "dismal-fronted pile of bastard Egyptian".

Manhattanites gather in 1881 to watch a true Egyptian obelisk being hoisted into place in Central Park. Dubbed "Cleopatra's Needle", the 70-foot-high stone monument actually had nothing at all to do with the famous queen. King Thutmose III ordered its construction in 1455 B.C. to honour the Sun God.

and grammar that was to be a standard work for some two centuries. In compiling his dictionary, Kircher made a wild guess that Coptic was akin to the language of ancient Egypt, a view that attracted scant attention until more than a century later.

The real breakthrough in solving the mystery of Egyptian hieroglyphs came as a by-product of 19th Century imperialism, and the accomplishment resulted from the activities of three men—one very famous, one moderately famous and one a nonentity. The first man was no less a personage than Napoleon; the second was the scholar Jean-François Champollion; the anonymous man was either a soldier or a labourer. In 1798, Napoleon launched an invasion of Egypt, and he included in his entourage a corps of 175 scholars and artists to study and record the wonders of their leader's latest conquest. The savants sent back to France a steady stream of reports, drawings and paintings of Egyptian relics, which, when published —some of them in a specially established periodical, *Courrier de l'Egypte*—aroused an enormous fascination with Egypt among European intellectuals. The impact of this new interest was pervasive: for a few years the salons of Paris and other great cities were swept by a wave of "Egyptian chic", in which Egyptian styles in garments and interior decoration became the rage.

Meantime, however, the conquerors were having their troubles: they came under attack from the Turkish army and from the British Mediterranean fleet. The French dug in at a number of sites, one of them near the town of Rosetta. There, in the summer of 1799, an unknown French soldier or Egyptian labourer, at work digging a trench, unearthed a slab of polished basalt covered entirely with carved writing —of three different kinds. One was hieroglyphic; one was a cursive script later labelled demotic; and, crucially, one was Greek. Here was a discovery indeed, for Greek was known to many of Napoleon's civilian experts—even to some of his generals.

They confronted their first bilingual inscription. The Greek text stated that the stone had been inscribed in the year 196 B.C. by the priests of Memphis. It expressed their gratitude to Ptolemy V, the King of Egypt, for his gifts to their temples, "which had increased the honours due to the King and his forefathers". Though no one could yet read the Egyptian characters, the presence of the Greek inscription side by side with the hieroglyphs brought Egyptian writing a great deal closer to being understood than it had ever been in modern times.

Copies of the inscriptions on the Rosetta stone were sent back to Europe, and scholars leaped upon them. One after another they tackled the new Egyptian find; one after another they gave up. Among the few to make any headway was David Akerblad, a Swedish scholar and diplomat; possessing a knowledge of Greek and Coptic, he made a promising start.

Coptic had become extinct in Egypt in the century and a half that had elapsed since Kircher had compiled his dictionary, but it survived as the liturgical language of the Coptic Christians (as it does today). By this time Kircher's conjecture that spoken Coptic derived from spoken Egyptian was beginning to gain acceptance, and it was known that the Coptic alphabet derived from the Greek alphabet.

A connection between Coptic and the hieroglyphs was visible in the inscription, though at first it eluded scholars. Thanks to its Egyptian origin, the spoken Coptic language contained sounds—such as "sh" —that the Greek alphabet could not express; and to denote these sounds the Greek-based Coptic alphabet borrowed seven symbols from the demotic script, which had evolved from hieroglyphs. Those facts meant that a somewhat tangled but traceable line could be drawn from Greek back to Coptic to demotic to hieroglyphs.

To 19th Century scholars who had their first look at the Egyptian writings, the tracing of that line was far in the future. But those among them who could read Greek and Coptic found familiar marks of both in the demotic script of the Rosetta stone, though no one could make sense of the hieroglyphs.

Akerblad, knowing Coptic and Greek, attacked the demotic script. Comparing it with the Greek text, he saw the proper names of Ptolemy Epiphanes (a pharaoh), Alexander (a Greek emperor), Alexandria (the capital of the Ptolemies) and Arsinoë (a name given to four princesses in the Ptolemaic Dynasty). He got so far as to pick them out in the demotic text. Examining these names more closely, he was able to find the equivalents of the Ls in Ptolemy and Alexander, the Ps in Ptolemy and Epiphanes, and so forth. But Akerblad progressed no further; discouraged, he failed to follow up the clues he had unearthed.

Meanwhile, the Rosetta stone had become the booty of war. Superior British naval power had forced the French to withdraw from Egypt, and to hand over all the treasures they had collected. The stone was shipped to the British Museum, where it remains.

There the inscriptions came to the attention of Thomas Young, an English physician and physicist, founder of the modern science of optics, whose avocation was dabbling in foreign languages. Knowing Greek, and acquainted with Akerblad's work on the Rosetta stone, Young managed to break down the demotic script into separate words, and then to match those words with their hieroglyphic counterparts. Young was the first to perceive that demotic, though a cursive script, had been derived from hieroglyphs.

Young's sharp eyes caught something else of importance: when the name of Ptolemy appeared in the hieroglyphs, it was enclosed in a cartouche, an oval band circumscribing the name. Knowing Ptolemy was a king, Young guessed—rightly—that the cartouche was a convention for indicating a royal name.

Such were the small steps that had been taken when the real hero of the battle to decipher Egyptian hieroglyphs entered the scene: the French genius Jean-François Champollion.

Champollion was marked from birth as an unusual child. His olive complexion, enormous dark eyes and thick, curly black hair were said to give him an Oriental appearance; while still a boy he was nicknamed "The Egyptian". So the story goes; surviving portraits of the great Egyptologist show a face that is swarthy but typically European. Champollion was a prodigy. At five he taught himself to read French by identifying words in his missal from prayers his mother had taught him to recite—a first exercise in decipherment. Soon he moved on to Greek and Latin, and at 11 he began studying Hebrew.

In that same year he had a momentous encounter with the great scientist Jean-Baptiste Fourier, a physicist and mathematician who had been one of Napoleon's experts in Egypt, whence he had brought back a small collection of ancient artifacts. Visiting young Champollion's school, Fourier fell into conver-

The Rosetta Stone: Key to the Puzzle of Egypt's Hieroglyphs

The Rosetta stone, inscribed in 196 B.C., carries one message in three different scripts glorifying Egypt's King Ptolemy V: in hieroglyphs (top), demotic (centre) and Greek.

While Napoleon's forces were invading Egypt, a slab of black basalt was accidentally dug up in 1799 near the town of Rosetta. On it were carved three kinds of writing: identifiable Greek with two different Egyptian scripts. The discovery created enormous interest in a Europe already fascinated by earlier Egyptian revelations (*pages 23-31*).

Although only nine at the time, a French boy named Jean-François Champollion was swept up in the excitement generated by the new finds —the ruins, the enigmatic inscriptions. Through school, he nurtured an extraordinary facility for languages and focused it on Egyptian writings. At 17, he was ready for the Rosetta stone. He studied Greek names of Egyptian rulers and, eventually, concluded that some hieroglyphs were phonetic, then tested that theory on as many Egyptian documents as he could find. His great work, only partly done, was cut short by a stroke in 1832. He was 42 when he died.

Jean-François Champollion sat for this portrait in 1830. Though admired for his brilliance, he was regarded as arrogant by his envious peers.

Found in 1815, this 26-foot monument had the name Cleopatra on it. The letters L P and T matched those in Ptolemy on the Rosetta stone, proving Champollion was on the right track.

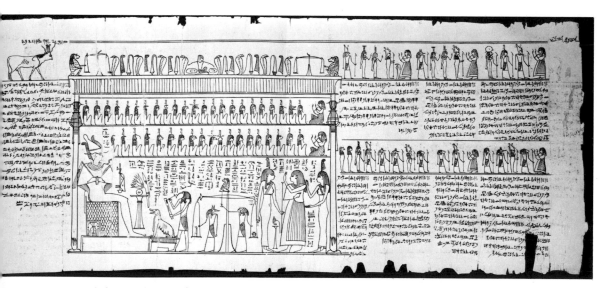

Columns of text in documents written on papyrus (above) also led Champollion, a compulsive Egyptologist, to identify hieratic, the script that evolved from hieroglyphs.

sation with the boy, was impressed by his obvious intelligence and invited him to examine the collection. Gazing at fragments of papyrus scrolls and stone tablets that were inscribed with hieroglyphs, Champollion asked whether anyone could read them. Fourier shook his head. "Then," the boy declared, according to legend, "I am going to do it."

It is a fact that the young prodigy's life was from then on increasingly focused on Egypt and its writing. Pausing only to write a book called *A History of Famous Dogs*—a childish account that began with Argus, the pet of the legendary Greek Odysseus and the creature that was first to welcome the hero home after 10 years of adventurous wandering—Champollion commenced at 13 to study the known languages of the Middle East: Arabic, Syrian, Aramaic, various ancient Persian dialects and—most importantly—Coptic. "I want to know Egyptian as well as I know French," he wrote at the time. "I am in fact a Copt who for his amusement translates into that language everything that comes into his head; I speak Coptic to myself so that no one will understand me." By 1809, already a professor of history at the Grenoble Academy, the 18-year-old Champollion knew Coptic well enough to keep a diary in that language.

In the same year, the young professor presented his first public report on Egyptian writing. By carefully comparing the two Egyptian inscriptions on the Rosetta stone with inscriptions on several papyrus scrolls that he had collected, Champollion had established that there were not two but three kinds of Egyptian writing: in addition to the hieroglyphic and the demotic, which were graven on the stone, there was a third script, now known as hieratic. It was cursive script that developed about 2900 B.C., not long after the first appearance of hieroglyphs, and was used for literary manuscripts and letters. Written with a brush on papyrus, the hieratic script turned out to have been used for 3,000 years. But because papyrus was perishable, relatively few examples exist, and they were hard to come by.

As anyone could, Champollion saw that the forms of each script were different, but he also perceived that all three expressed the same words—that each script was equivalent to the others, in the sense that every sign in one inscription corresponded to a sign in each of the others. Therefore, any clues to the interpretation of one script would be almost automatically applicable to the other two.

Champollion now devoted himself to drawing up a systematic catalogue of all the hieroglyphic signs in all the inscriptions he could get hold of, and to tabulating their hieratic and demotic equivalents. In the course of this task, he turned up a demotic sign that appeared to be almost identical to one already familiar to him from his knowledge of Coptic. Coptic had a vaguely Y-shaped symbol, called a *fai*, that stood for the sound "f" and was used as a suffix on nouns to denote "him" and "his". Champollion saw that wherever "him" or "his" appeared in the Rosetta stone's Greek inscription, the corresponding passage in the demotic text had a character resembling the Coptic *fai* at the end of a word. He concluded that the symbol must be a suffix denoting "him" or "his" in Egyptian (as in Coptic) and that because of its likeness to the Coptic letter, it must be sounded as "f". He was right. The discovery confirmed Kircher's hunch of 150 years before: that Coptic was a descendant of the ancient Egyptian language.

Champollion made another observation that put

him on the threshold of deciphering the hieroglyphs, though he did not suspect it. He noted that wherever the character resembling the Coptic *fai* appeared in the demotic text, the corresponding passage in the hieroglyphs showed a picture of a viper with two horns. But remaining under the spell of the mystique that had bemused Horapollo and Kircher, Champollion still supposed that the signs stood for entire words, not sounds, so he failed to hit on the reason for the viper. He did not know that the word for viper in Egyptian happened to be *fy*—and he did not guess that the snake was used to signify the sound "f" in the passage he was trying to read.

Nonetheless, through noting the correspondence of such symbols as the demotic *fai* and the viper, Champollion had by 1821 made enough progress to be able to transliterate demotic inscriptions into hieroglyphic or hieratic, and vice versa.

Then Champollion was seized by a simple, revolutionary inspiration: he counted the number of words in the Greek text on the Rosetta stone and the number of signs in the hieroglyphic text. The number of hieroglyphs exceeded the number of Greek words by three to one. But if, as he had to assume, the two texts related the same message, then there were too many hieroglyphs for each one to represent a word. The conclusion he drew was that some of the hieroglyphs *must* represent sounds, not words.

Getting back to fundamentals, Champollion now turned to the Rosetta stone cartouche that Young and Akerblad had translated as "Ptolemy". The cartouche contained seven different signs. If each figure stood for a different sound, Champollion reasoned that he would now have phonetic values for seven signs. But how to check his theory? The key turned up quite un-

expectedly. In January 1822, Champollion got hold of another bilingual Greek and hieroglyphic inscription known (from the Greek) to contain the name of Cleopatra. And Cleopatra, as Champollion realized with excitement, contained many of the same letters as Ptolemy. Quickly he looked through the new inscription, and located "Cleopatra" in its cartouche. There, exactly where he had expected, were symbols corresponding to those in Ptolemy.

As he later reported to the French Academy: "The second sign, a reclining lion, which would give the L in Cleopatra, is exactly the same as the fourth sign in the name of Ptolemy, also an L. The fifth symbol in Cleopatra, which must represent the P, is the first sign in the hieroglyphic name Ptolemy."

Pushing on, Champollion successfully applied such phonetic values to every name he found in dozens of Egyptian inscriptions, on obelisks and on papyri: the pharaohs Thutmose and Ramses; the Roman emperors Tiberius, Domitian and Trajan; Alexander the Great; Berenice (queen of one of the many Ptolemies). He also worked out sound values in such titles as Autokrator, Greek for "emperor".

Champollion found that the symbols were different from alphabetic letters; used in combinations that varied from word to word and from text to text, they made hieroglyphic writing a hodgepodge of consonants, syllables and determinatives—symbols that serve to clarify word meanings (*pages 44-45*). Nevertheless he had proved that writing in Egypt had been a highly developed tool since 3000 B.C.

Champollion suddenly died of a stroke at the age of 42; he had never been healthy, and right to the end he worked like a man possessed. Because inevitably he made some mistakes, and also perhaps

A Quick Lesson in Reading Hieroglyphs

To help decipher the various symbols in Egyptian hieroglyphic script, scholars divide the signs into three groups.

Ideograms are pictures of actual things referred to, or of related ideas; for example, the sky ideogram in the key below stands for both "sky" and "heaven". *Phonograms* indicate one, two or three consonant sounds (ancient Egyptian writing contained no vowels) based on the rebus principle; the phonogram of a basket specifies the sounds "n b", pronounced, roughly, "neb". *Determinatives* clarify the meanings of accompanying symbols; thus a seated goddess in conjunction with the phonogram for "s t" indicates a goddess' name.

Written during the 13th Century B.C., the inscription at the right concerns the goddess Aset. It contains examples of all three types of signs: ideograms, phonograms and determinatives. Egyptologists suggest that the passage—with approximations of missing vowels supplied—would have been recited *Aset, Weret, Mut Netcher, Nebet Pet*. Translated, and using the goddess' more familiar Greek name, the words mean "Isis, Great Female, Mother of the God, Mistress of Heaven".

IDEOGRAMS

- Cloth around a pole: emblem for "god"
- Stylized sky: "heaven"

PHONOGRAMS

- Mouth: stands for "r"
- Loaf of bread: "t"
- Throne: "s t"
- Swallow: "w r"
- Vulture: "m t"
- Basket: "n b"
- Cloth wrapped around a pole: "n t r"

DETERMINATIVES

- Seated goddess: means "female deity"
- An egg: "femininity"

In this first of four bracketed groups of hieroglyphs, the throne phonogram indicates the sounds "s t"; the half-circular bread loaf, another phonogram, reinforces the "t" sound and serves to suggest femininity. The egg and seated figure are determinatives for a female name and for "goddess". The four symbols, therefore, with the addition of vowel sounds, form the name *Aset*, Egyptian for:

ISIS

In the second group, a swallow serves a double function, indicating both the idea "great" and the sounds "w r". The mouth phonogram reinforces the "r", while the bread loaf adds the sound "t", and also connotes femininity. Together, this cluster of phonograms signifies the characterization *Weret*:

GREAT FEMALE

In the third group of signs, the vulture, a rebus for "mother", is a phonogram for "m t"; the "t" sound is reinforced by the bread loaf. The emblem of a cloth wrapped around a pole serves a dual purpose: an ideogram for a deity and a phonogram for the sounds "n t r". The symbols can be read as *Mut Netcher*:

MOTHER OF THE GOD

In the fourth group, a basket phonogram, pronounced "n b", means "master". The bread loaf below it adds a "t" and, again, signifies "femininity". The sky ideogram at bottom means "heaven", and also suggests the consonants "p t". Combined, these signs communicate to the reader one of Isis' grandest titles, *Nebet Pet*:

MISTRESS OF HEAVEN

Queen Nefertari presents two bowls to the goddess Isis. Both are surrounded by inscriptions, one of which (arrow) is analysed opposite.

because his views were ahead of his time, scholars lacking his intuition dismissed his work for some 20 years after his death. But Champollion was right far more often than he was wrong, and today it is generally held that the foundation of all that is known about the Egyptian language was laid by the brilliant Frenchman who first read the Rosetta stone.

Though deciphering hieroglyphs was complicated enough—the language being extinct, the links to modern times all but broken—that job was easy compared with the task that scholars confronted in cuneiform, the script that arose in Mesopotamia.

To a 17th- or 18th-Century scholar, Mesopotamia might well have seemed an implausible site for the birth of writing. The land possessed few visible ancient monuments and few cities, and it was as impoverished as any place on earth. Some legendary names survived in literature and lore: the Assyrians, the Babylonians and the Elamites figured in the Bible, but hardly more than the names were known to Europeans. The languages had vanished; the palaces and temples had been reduced by time and conquest to bleak mounds of earth and rubble on which a few goats and sheep found sparse pasture.

East of Mesopotamia lay Persia—modern Iran. Europeans familiar with Herodotus knew that Persia had once been the site of rich and mighty civilizations, and that the Persian rulers Darius and Xerxes had very nearly conquered Greece. But beyond those few facts they knew very little.

From the 15th to the 19th Century, as trade and travel penetrated ever farther east from Europe, a succession of wayfarers beheld many a sight that aroused their curiosity—and some of them reported their sense of wonder. The earliest such reports on record are those of Pietro della Valle, a wealthy Neapolitan who set out on a pilgrimage to the Holy Land in 1614, and ended up making a 12-year journey through Turkey, Egypt, Mesopotamia, Persia and India. The Neapolitan sent vivid and entertaining letters back to friends. In one of these messages he included a drawing of some curious carvings consisting of wedge-shaped marks he had seen on the pillars in the vast ruins of Persepolis in southwestern Persia. Pietro della Valle assumed that the carvings were writing, but he could find no clue to their meaning.

Around the beginning of the 18th Century, Engelbert Kämpfer, a German traveller to Persepolis, viewed the same inscriptions and christened them *litterae cuneatae*—"wedge-shaped letters", from which comes the modern English word "cuneiform".

In 1765 Carsten Niebuhr, a young man from Holstein, now part of Germany, arrived in Persepolis at the end of a harrowing expedition in which all five of his companions had succumbed to disease. Niebuhr made detailed sketches of the ruins and copied out the full text of several inscriptions. While doing so, he noticed something that previous viewers of the inscriptions had missed: there were significant differences between the inscriptions, suggesting they recorded three different languages. Niebuhr came to this realization because, though all the characters were formed of wedges, they were arranged in different combinations (*page 48*).

Over the next century, these and other travellers to Mesopotamia came upon more inscriptions on ruined walls and interspersed among rock carvings; here and there, they discovered clay tablets lying about in the sand. From the fragments they drew conclusions that gave future scholars a base from which to start when deciphering began in earnest in the 19th Century. The most important piece of information the travellers established was that the ruins at Persepolis had once been a ceremonial capital of the Persian Empire and that the inscriptions there dated from the Achemenid Dynasty (559-331 B.C.).

This was a vital clue for two reasons. First, the deeds of the Achemenids were recorded by Herodotus, and that gave scholars some names to look for among the finds. Second, it could now be assumed that at least one of the three inscriptions would be in Old Persian, the prevailing language in the Persian Empire. But since the Persians had conquered many peoples, the population of the empire had been multilingual; some Persian subjects spoke Elamite, the tongue of a people cited in the Bible; others spoke Akkadian, the language of the defunct Babylonian Empire. Official proclamations were inscribed in all three languages.

Attempts at deciphering cuneiform were desultory until 1802, when Georg Friedrich Grotefend, a German high school teacher, accepted a dare from a friend: find the key to the Persepolis inscriptions. Grotefend was not an Oriental scholar, but he was a teacher of Greek, and he had a fortunate bent for acrostics and other word puzzles.

Grotefend felt sure that the writing at Persepolis had something to do with the kings who had reigned there, because the texts resembled later Persian inscriptions accompanied by Greek translations found at another site. The Greek versions of these inscriptions contained the repetitive formula "X, Great King, King of Kings, Son of Y, Great King". Armed

with this knowledge, and aware that this formula remained much the same from century to century and place to place, Grotefend took a shot in the dark. Why not, he asked, assume that the Persepolis inscriptions included the same formula?

Indeed, he found a group of signs there that occurred again and again, and assumed that the group formed a word meaning "king". Peering more closely he saw what were apparently the names of a succession of kings, set down so that they read something like this: X, Great King, King of Kings, Son of Y, Great King, King of Kings, Son of Z.

And there, staring Grotefend in the face, was a clue to the actual identities of these kings: X was a king and the son of a king; Y, his father, was a king but Z, Y's father and X's grandfather, was *not* a king.

To supply the missing piece of the puzzle—an identifiable break in a dynastic line—Grotefend now needed three names from Persian history: a father, son and grandson of whom only the last two had been kings. He found them in Herodotus' list of the Achemenid monarchs and their genealogy: Hystaspes, a provincial governor under Cyrus the Great, fathered King Darius, who fathered King Xerxes.

After only a few months' work, Grotefend had won his dare; he had found the cuneiform signs for the words "king", "great" and "son", and for three proper names that loomed large in Persian history. Reading the language in full was still a long way off, but Grotefend had got the process underway. There, for all practical purposes, he stopped. Though for years thereafter he continued to pick away at cuneiform, he never succeeded in actually reading more than a few words or phrases. Academic notice of his achievement came slowly and reluctantly (as a mere schoolteacher, he had insufficient rank in a world dominated by university professors). But the ground he had broken was recognized by later scholars.

The inscription that Grotefend had worked on was Fifth Century B.C. Old Persian cuneiform, the most recent and the simplest of what turned out to be four major varieties of cuneiform. The Elamite and Babylonian that appeared with it at Persepolis were more difficult. And there remained the fourth, which had not even been discovered yet. Their solutions have required the collaborative labours of a dozen scholars down to the present day.

One of the greatest and most colourful of these savants was Henry Creswicke Rawlinson, a British cavalry major and diplomat who first went to India in 1826 as an enlisted man to serve the burgeoning British Empire. There he studied Hindustani, Arabic and modern Persian. During a later diplomatic tour of duty in Persia, he took up cuneiform. With only the sketchiest knowledge of Grotefend's earlier work, Rawlinson first duplicated and then quickly overtook Grotefend, achieving a virtually complete translation of the Old Persian portion of the Persepolis inscriptions, a feat that he accomplished with his wide knowledge of languages, his sense of linguistic correspondence and the help of Herodotus' work.

But for all his learning and intelligence, Rawlinson was handicapped by the brevity of the Old Persian cuneiform inscriptions at his disposal. It is one thing for a decipherer to pick out the meaning of a few words in a tomb inscription no longer than a modern picture caption, and quite another to grasp the full range of the language in which it is written. Rawlinson filled the gap by finding the longest cuneiform

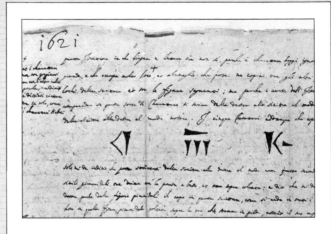

Pietro della Valle, travelling in Persepolis, neatly copied the cuneiform characters at the top in a letter he sent home to Italy in 1621. The first examples of cuneiform ever published in Europe, these signs intrigued and frustrated would-be decipherers, including Della Valle —although he correctly deduced that the script read from left to right. The longer sample at the bottom, from the same site, reached Europe in 1694. It was copied by Engelbert Kämpfer, who clambered over the lofty ruins, risking sunstroke and broken limbs, to view the characters; he was the first to label the script cuneiform, a name based on the Latin word cuneus, "wedge".

inscription yet—a trilingual carved on a mountain-side during the reign of Darius. He then performed an extraordinary feat of cliff-hanging acrobatics, risking his own life while copying the inscription.

Near the little town of Behistun in western Persia, a great mountain of stone overlooks the ancient road from the Iranian plateau to the Mesopotamian valley lands. Well over 300 feet above the road are carved heroic relief figures celebrating the deeds of Darius. Below the sculptures are several wide panels bearing a carved inscription—about 1,200 lines in all—in three different scripts and languages: one in Old Persian, and the other two in Elamite and Babylonian.

Rawlinson copied the lower lines of the Old Persian inscription by standing on a narrow ledge just below it. But to reach the upper portion, he needed a ladder—and the ledge was so narrow that mounting a ladder on it was a risky prospect. Rawlinson found himself, by his account, "standing on the topmost step of the ladder, with no other support than steadying the body against the rock with the left arm, while the left hand holds the notebook, and the right hand is employed with the pencil". And thus perilously perched, he reported, "I copied all the upper inscriptions, and the interest of the occupation entirely did away with any sense of danger".

The second of the three inscriptions posed an even chancier problem, for at that point on the cliff the ledge was missing below it—though it resumed farther along the mountain face. Rawlinson tried to use his ladder as a bridge across the gap in the ledge. The two existing strips of the ledge were so narrow, however, and the ladder was so flimsy that it split and part of it went crashing down over the precipice. Rawlinson managed to hang on to the cliff and thus save himself. Eventually he constructed a more durable bridge and successfully copied the Elamite inscription. Subsequently, he described these experiences as "such as any person with ordinary nerves may successfully encounter"—a judgment that most people would consider a remarkable understatement.

When he tackled the third and most inaccessible inscription, he found it "quite beyond my powers of climbing to reach". Even the local tribesmen, though "accustomed to track the mountain goats over the entire face of the mountain", declared it unreachable. At length, Rawlinson enlisted the aid of "a wild Kurdish boy", who managed to squeeze himself up a cleft in the rock to the left of the inscription, then drive a stout wooden peg into the cleft, attach a rope to the peg, cross the face of the inscription to another cleft on the right side, drive in another peg and tie the other end of the rope to it. He attached a sort of bosun's chair to the rope strung between the pegs on either side of the inscription. Working from this rig, the boy then made a papier-mâché cast under Rawlinson's direction.

"The method of forming these paper casts is exceedingly simple," Rawlinson reported. It required only that scraps of moistened absorbent paper be stuffed into the inscriptions, and then beaten "into the crevices with a stout brush, adding as many layers of paper as it may be wished to give consistency to the cast. The paper is left there to dry, and on being taken off it exhibits a perfect impression of the writing." No doubt. But how did the boy hoist himself, along with enough paper and liquid and the stout brush, 300 feet into the air? And where did he stow his equipment while he worked? Did Rawlinson help or only give directions? With understatement in inverse proportion to his determination, Rawlinson neglected to say.

Using the lengthy trilingual he now had in his possession—along with several others that had turned up meantime—Rawlinson and other scholars thought they could employ the Old Persian text he had deciphered to help them work on the other two. At first, the Elamite script looked as though it should not be unduly difficult, because it consisted of only about 110 signs, most of them apparently representing syllables and the rest standing for words.

But none of them resembled any of the signs used in Old Persian. What was worse, the Elamite language revealed no similarity to any known tongue. Even to this day, after more than a century of work, Elamite has been only partially deciphered.

The third script, in Babylonian, initially posed an even more intractable problem. Its signs numbered several hundred, and that meant that many of them must denote words, though there was a confusing array of symbols that were clearly phonetic, chiefly in the proper names of Darius and other eminent figures. That led scholars to the mistaken conclusion that among the characters were alphabetic letters. After years of frustrating efforts, Rawlinson wrote, "I despaired of ever obtaining a satisfactory result".

But help was on the way, as other scholars were becoming interested in cuneiform. One was the Reverend Edward Hincks, a shy, bespectacled theologian from Ireland. Hincks determined that the Babylonian phonetic signs were not alphabetic but syllabic —combining consonants and vowels. Thus seven different signs, all of which earlier scholars had thought stood for the letter R, in fact stood for the syllables ar, ir, er, ur, and ra, ri and ru. Hincks further

discovered that Babylonian cuneiform, like Egyptian writing, sometimes used the same sign as a phonetic symbol, a word sign or a determinative, depending on the context.

Hincks's findings were encouraging in one respect, since they pointed the road to the proper understanding of the phonetic signs, but they introduced another element of ambiguity into an already baffling script.

Indeed, Rawlinson was encountering the same kinds of confusion on his own. In 1851, after examining a number of inscriptions from different places, Rawlinson demonstrated that sometimes a single phonetic sign might stand for not one but several syllables—in one case, as different as lul, lib, lub, pakh and nar. Soon it was realized that the converse was also true: several different signs could represent one and the same syllable; the extreme case was the syllable du, which—scholars eventually found—could be written in no fewer than 23 ways.

This revelation seemed to make no sense. If the same sign could stand for any one of several different sounds, while the same sound might be represented by any one of several different signs, how on earth could anybody be certain what the writings meant? Challenged by sceptics who suggested that the decipherers were bogged down, members of the Royal Asiatic Society in 1857 contrived a test that they hoped would confirm the soundness of scholarly work already done. Having obtained a new cuneiform text on some clay documents just excavated at a 12th Century B.C. Assyrian site, the society submitted copies to Rawlinson, Hincks and two other well-known cuneiform scholars, asking them to translate the text independently and return their results in sealed envelopes. Six weeks later, a commit-

Georg Grotefend, the German high school teacher who first deciphered Old Persian to win a dare in 1802, had trouble getting his achievement recognized because he lacked academic status. However, he was a highly educated man who possessed a profound knowledge of the classics, a taste for word puzzles and a flexible mind—a combination of talents and skills that helped lead to his great discovery.

tee of the society opened the envelopes—and all four translations, though differing in detail, proved alike in their essential respects—a fact that surprised and silenced the doubters.

There were many reasons for the interchangeability of cuneiform signs. One is the fact that over long centuries of use both spoken sounds and written symbols evolve—and they do so at different rates of speed. Different generations speak differently, but retain the written conventions of their fathers; new words arise to express new thoughts, and old characters take on new functions even as they continue to perform the old ones. While the effects of such an evolution might seem puzzling at first glance, the matter is easily explained by analogy to English—which has come a long way in both sound and appearance since Chaucer's day, even since Shakespeare's era and, for that matter, since George Washington's. Cuneiform, it must be remembered, lived in the East for more than 3,000 years.

Two other facts about cuneiform became apparent to the 19th Century scholars who studied it. One was that Akkadian, the language spoken by the Babylonians, was Semitic. (It proved to have resemblances to such Semitic languages as Hebrew and Arabic.) The other was that the Babylonian script was not, as first thought, the oldest version of cuneiform, but was itself descended from some as yet unknown forbear.

That thought was first voiced by Hincks, who deduced it from a huge gap: the lack, in the cuneiform scripts he was studying, of apparent rational connection between the appearances of word signs and phonetic signs. In Egyptian, nearly all the phonetic hieroglyphs could be shown to have originated as pictorial word signs. Later, through the rebus principle, a sign came to stand for the sound of the word it pictured, or part of the word. In cuneiform, however, almost none of the wedge marks showed any pictorial relationship to the words they stood for in Persian, Elamite or Babylonian. Hincks assumed that if cuneiform characters had originated as word pictures, like the phonetic Egyptian hieroglyphs, then the words they had originally stood for must have belonged to some older language, now lost.

Hincks was right. Before long, Rawlinson addressed himself to a new cache of clay tablets. They were obviously written in cuneiform—the characters had the now-familiar wedge-shaped marks—though they could not be read as Old Persian, Elamite or Akkadian. But among the tablets were some containing long lists—and on examination they turned out to be the equivalent of dictionaries. They showed Akkadian words paired with unfamiliar words in the cuneiform script. The new-found language was, after a long dispute, eventually named Sumerian. The people who spoke it had settled in southern Mesopotamia at some unknown date, perhaps a millennium and a half or more before the Akkadians, their neighbours to the north, came to dominate the region. The Akkadians adapted the Sumerian cuneiform letters to their own, quite different language.

The decipherment of Sumerian appeared in some respects to be an easier undertaking than had been the understanding of the later cuneiform scripts. Not only did the clay tablet word lists provide a start, but continuing excavations yielded quantities of bilingual inscriptions in which Sumerian words were translated line by line into Akkadian.

For all that, decipherment of the earliest-known script was difficult; Sumerian had no linguistic affinities with any known language. Its grammar bore certain resemblances to that of Turkish, Hungarian and Finnish, but its vocabulary was unique. So baffling did Sumerian inscriptions prove that no translations appeared until 1905—half a century after Rawlinson and Hincks had discovered many of the peculiarities in the language already mentioned—and no systematic Sumerian grammar appeared until 1923. To this day, Sumerologists must insert blanks and question marks into their translations a great deal more often than they would like.

Enough has been worked out, however, to support an assumption that the Sumerians were the inventors of cuneiform. The Sumerians also have the strongest claim to being the inventors of writing itself. Although some earlier clay tablets bearing numerical notations have been found in Syria and Iran, Sumerian tablets, which go back to 3100 B.C., are the oldest found anywhere with full writing. The earliest Sumerian scripts are pictographic; over a period of time the pictographic signs evolve into arbitrary phonetic signs. These are the characters that the Akkadians took over and bequeathed to their heirs, the Babylonians and Assyrians.

As archaeologists proceeded to excavate the dusty mounds of Mesopotamia—all that remained of once-flourishing cities—more and more evidence of a high civilization with a rich and varied literature came to light, much of which neither classical historians nor the Bible had given any hint of. Even with this new evidence, years of labour by many other scholars were necessary to piece together the story of how writing had come to be devised in the first place, and to assemble a picture of the Sumerian society in which written language had arisen.

Intrepid Explorers on a Scholarly Quest

The final decipherment of cuneiform was the work of decades, and depended on the contributions of scholars from many countries. But before they could start their labours, other men no less learned risked life and limb to find the cuneiform inscriptions and copy them. The quest was perilous for a number of reasons.

The inscriptions were located in the Middle East, at the time a region still a mystery to Europeans. At every step, the searchers faced death from bandits, fanatic Muslim tribesmen and virulent diseases. And the inscriptions, once discovered, were often virtually inaccessible.

In this arduous advance work, two men achieved special distinction. In the 18th Century, after losing five travelling companions to disease, a German, Carsten Niebuhr, made the first accurate copies of cuneiform at Persepolis, an ancient capital of Persia. For Sir Henry Rawlinson, a 19th Century Englishman, the only way to copy the largest cuneiform inscription yet found was to cling to a sheer cliff in Persia, working 300 hair-raising feet above the ground.

In an engraving from Carsten Niebuhr's account of his journey, the author stands proudly in the costume given him by an Arab ruler. Usually, Niebuhr travelled about dressed as a poor man to avoid any trouble with the sort of bloodthirsty tribesmen shown fighting each other in the background.

Amid Palatial Ruins, a Journey's Reward

Carsten Niebuhr, a poor farmer's son who was educated late in life, became staff mathematician of a six-man expedition commissioned in 1756 by the Danish king: the group had the broad assignment of exploring Arabia "for the advancement of knowledge".

The expedition's ultimate place in history was to rest on extraordinary drawings made by Niebuhr at Persepolis. He arrived there a sick man, as the consequence of a series of tragic accidents. Fleeing the deserts of Arabia, where two of the group had died of malaria, the four survivors—all ailing themselves—took ship to Bombay. Two died at sea, and a third soon after their arrival. Alone, Niebuhr debated whether to return to Denmark by boat or to risk the long and dangerous journey overland. He decided on a land route by way of Persia and —often racked with malaria—arrived at Persepolis in 1765.

There, as he had done throughout his travels, he painstakingly sketched what he saw, this time the ruins and the cuneiform inscriptions he found all about him. In the course of his task, Niebuhr was the first to realize that the inscriptions involved three different cuneiform scripts.

He finally returned to Copenhagen in 1767 and, five years later, published the first of his five works. His detailed drawings provided scholars with the raw material to solve the meaning of at least one of the three languages recorded at Persepolis: Old Persian.

Niebuhr's trials were not over however. Reflected glare from the polished stone of the ruins had damaged his eyes so badly that for the last few years of his life, until his death in 1815 at 82, he was totally blind.

In this Niebuhr rendering of a bas-relief at a Persepolis palace, a procession of representatives

This Niebuhr drawing concentrates on the free-standing walls and disembodied portals that once opened on the palaces, halls and courtyards of Persepolis.

Captioned in Dutch and French, a page (right) from one of Niebuhr's books combined two elements: an engraving, copied from a staircase, of a lion attacking a bull; and at far right, the 42 symbols (separated by dots) that Niebuhr isolated, guessing that they included signs of a syllabic alphabet.

55

from Persia's subject nations lines up to offer tribute to King Darius. Niebuhr faithfully reproduced their different clothing, headgear and armour.

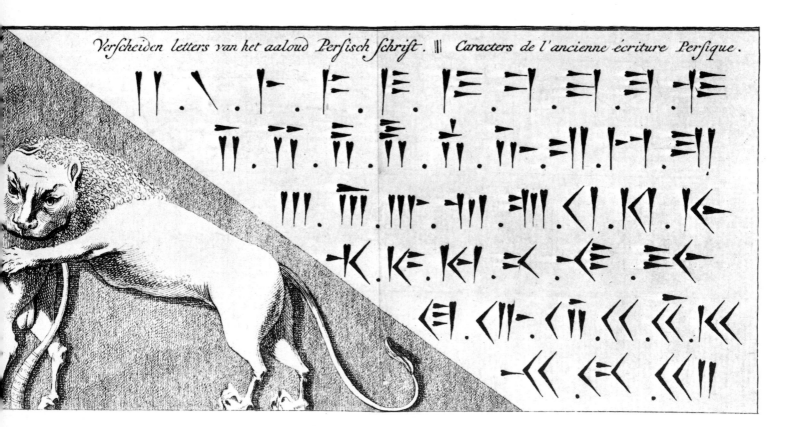

Verscheiden letters van het aaloud Persisch schrift. ‖ Caracters de l'ancienne écriture Persique.

A Giant Clue on a Cliffside

In 1835, a 25-year-old English officer employed as a military advisor to a Persian official stood at the base of a precipice at Behistun in the Zagros Mountains of Iran. He scanned the cliff eagerly for toe holds to assist his climb to a huge cuneiform inscription—written in Old Persian, Babylonian and Elamite—that stretched up the rock high above him. During the next few years Sir Henry Rawlinson, an athlete-scholar who wrote of his love for "pigeon-shooting, pig-sticking and steeple-chasing", perched on ledges, clung to overhangs and balanced on ladders to copy the ancient message.

Rawlinson had realized that the inscriptions, even today the longest trilingual ever found in cuneiform, were a key to understanding the three ancient languages they expressed. By 1847 he had completed the translation of Old Persian and was working on the Elamite version; by 1851 he had established meanings for 200 signs in Babylonian. With Babylonian largely understood, the thousands of cuneiform tablets being found in Mesopotamia—embodying secrets of some of the world's oldest civilizations—finally could be read.

The Behistun rock, with its monumental carving, towers over the Iranian plain.

Sir Henry Rawlinson (left) made the first copy of the carving at Behistun (below). The bas-relief (shown in detail overleaf), which is surrounded by the trilingual inscriptions, summarizes King Darius's Sixth Century B.C. victories. With one foot on his most hated enemy, Gaumata—a rival for the Persian throne —the King judges nine others, roped together with their hands tied. Behind the King are two officers bearing the royal lance and bow. Floating over the whole scene is the Persian chief god, Ahuramazda, who helped Darius because, according to the King's words, "I was not a follower of the lie, I was not a doer of wrong". Before Rawlinson's translation, some scholars had supposed that the scene represented the captive tribes of Israel.

Scale of Feet.

C. 10.

A. 18.

A. 10.

C. 10.

C. 5.

8785

B. 2.

B. 7.

b. 3.

c. 3.

Key Sketch showing the dimensions
on the face of the great sculptured
Italic Capit.
Old English.
Small Ital.
Mem. The Median Tablet of 10 lines marked C. is unace.

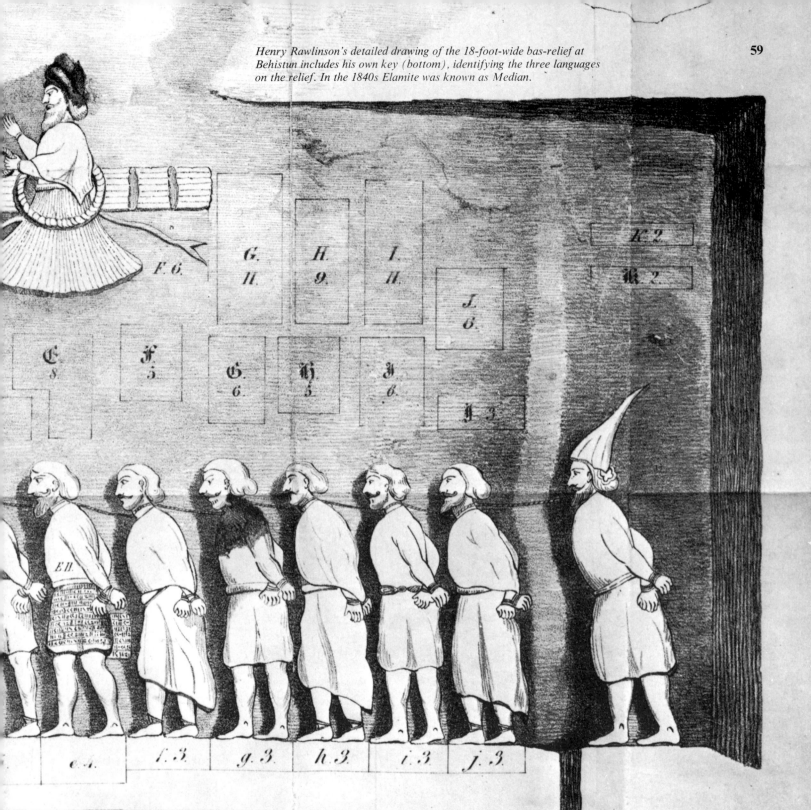

Henry Rawlinson's detailed drawing of the 18-foot-wide bas-relief at Behistun includes his own key (bottom), identifying the three languages on the relief. In the 1840s Elamite was known as Median.

ve positions of the figures and detached trilingual inscriptions
Behistun together with the number of lines contained in each inscription.
  C &c) denote the Persian Tablets.
. C &c.) mark the Median Translations.
. b c &c.) are attached to the Babylonian Transcripts.
v a Transcript in the other languages and the Babylonian translations of A & K are also wanting

By the time pictorial forms of writing appeared in the Middle East, between 3500 and 3000 B.C., *Homo sapiens* had had the power of speech for at least 30,000 years. For nearly as long, men had possessed the basic skills required for writing: the ability to draw pictures and to count and record numbers. Yet they had made do with only the simplest means of conveying information: notched tally sticks, knotted cords and random pictures.

Then during the next six centuries (3100 to 2500 B.C.), they devised comprehensive and sophisticated systems for keeping records and sending messages. How did the invention of writing first come about, and what course did it then follow?

From the plough to the lunar rocket, inventions arise because they satisfy or ease the needs and desires of a society—and such was the case with writing. As the first communities grew larger, the relationships among their people grew more remote, more conflicting, less trusting: the need intensified for a form of communication that would overcome distances, clearly record the obligations of man towards man and towards the community, and help organize large social projects.

Without exception, the earliest literate societies arose along the banks of great rivers: the Nile, the Tigris and the Euphrates, the Indus, and the Huang-Ho. In the valleys of all these rivers, rainfall during the growing season ranges from scant (the Huang-Ho) to virtually non-existent (the Nile). The same rivers annually overflow their banks, fertilizing the valley lands with silt. But the floods also menace man and his works. The Huang-Ho, which is known in the West as the Yellow River for the enormous load of yellow silt it deposits, is also known as "China's sorrow" for the grief its uncontrolled floods can bring.

Utilizing the benefits of the rivers—and neutralizing their threats—required co-operation among the peoples who lived along river banks. Farmers needed irrigation canals to carry water to the fields as a supplement for scarce rain, and they had to build dikes and diversion channels to shunt the flood waters away from heavily settled areas. Such projects were possible only with the large-scale, organized efforts of whole villages or groups of villages, whose inhabitants were answerable to administrators. The administrators, in turn, depended on taxation for the financing, and a system of taxation cannot be efficiently operated without a method of keeping accounts and a way of planning ahead.

Such were the pressures and requirements that impelled the ancient world towards the evolution of writing. To visualize the process in detail, imagine the history of a town along the lower Euphrates in Mesopotamia—sketched here in a series of vignettes developed by analysis of archaeological findings, by reasoning backwards through written documents of later periods and by drawing analogies to living societies. The scenario covers the town's history over a period of about two millennia, from 4000 B.C., a time when writing was not yet known, to 2000 B.C., when writing had become a fulcrum of civilized life and was in use all over the Middle East.

A silver vessel dedicated by the Sumerian king Entemena of Lagash to Ningirsu, the god of rainstorms and floods, is rimmed with a Sumerian inscription listing the King's various titles. Dating from the Third Millennium B.C., the piece is engraved with successive winged figures of lion-headed eagles, symbolizing the god's restless and violent spirit.

About 4000 B.C., the town numbers perhaps 4,000 people. Despite its modest size, it is the commercial and religious centre for a cluster of little villages, scattered up and down the banks of the river and its winding secondary channels, over a radius of perhaps five miles. Upstream and downstream lie other such clusters, spaced 20 to 30 miles apart, each centred on its own market town. Between them lie reed-filled swamps, where scattered bands of tribesmen trap fish and waterfowl; in the same areas, adjacent dry grasslands provide the villagers with pasture for their sheep, goats and cattle.

Within the town and its satellite villages, nearly all the population lives by farming—raising crops of wheat, barley, lentils, onions and cucumbers. Come spring, the farmers dig up the ground with heavy hoes, break the clods by turning the cattle into the field and sow seeds in holes made with pointed sticks.

Hardly are the seeds planted before floodtime approaches. The men of each village must check the primitive dikes that surround their fields—here repairing a baffle of reed matting, there strengthening a weak place with earth brought in on ox-drawn sledges. In time, as the river waters recede, the farmers periodically open narrow cuts in the dikes and let water into the fields to nourish the burgeoning crops.

The farmers keep no records of any sort; there is no need. To inventory their modest possessions, they have only to run their eyes around their reed and mud huts. If a man's hoe breaks and he must borrow one from a neighbour, he does so as casually as his wife borrows a few onions or a bowl of curds. Everyone knows everyone else—and everyone else's business; a man or woman who sought to escape a debt or other obligation would be censured by most of the community.

When the farmers' crops mature, it is time to go to market. Every few days one or two villagers take the road to town, each driving an ox-drawn sledge bearing a sack of grain or lentils, and perhaps a bundle of fleece. In the town marketplace, they swap these commodities for goods offered by the town craftsmen and merchants: a few yards of colourfully dyed cloth to be made into festive clothing, a pot handsomely painted in blue and white, a flint hoe-blade to replace one that has been broken or a couple of ceramic sickle blades, which only the town potter is skilful enough to fire to the hard, glassy edge that will chop through the tough stalks of wheat and barley.

None of these transactions need be recorded, since they are normally conducted on a simple barter basis. Occasionally a seller may extend a modest, easily remembered amount of credit to someone he has dealt with all his life.

After bargaining and gossiping, the farmers do not forget to visit the temple, a low building of mud brick that stands impressively on a 15-foot mound. There they make an offering of some of their goods, and perhaps consult the presiding priest or one of his three or four assistants on what to do about a case of sickness in the family, a quarrel with a neighbour, or a married daughter who has produced no son.

The head priest is the most consequential person in the town, and indeed in the whole cluster of villages. Not only is he a principal member of the town's council of elders, who resolve important disputes and organize the common defence against the raiders that descend on the town and surrounding villages periodically from the mountains or desert, but he is also deep in the councils of the gods, who nourish the fields when they are properly propitiated—and who may unleash a merciless flood to sweep away an entire village when offended.

The temple also serves practical functions. If a farmer's crops have been blighted, or swept away by a storm god, the priest will dispense seed for a second sowing from the temple's ranked jars of offerings. The amount of seed to be lent is notched on a tally stick, which is then split up the middle; half goes with the borrower and the other half, with its matching notches, remains in the temple. At harvest time, the farmer will return the loan and his half of the tally stick to be matched with the half that the priest kept. Of course, the farmer will add a handsome offering to show his gratitude for the gods' help. Should the man be unlucky enough to lose the second crop as well, he may have to give the gods part of his land or one of his children.

The temple also serves as a sort of safe deposit for the town's merchants. Two or three times a year, a group of merchants will form a caravan to visit the mountain tribes in the hill country to the north, there to trade barley and wheat for the high-quality stone the town craftsmen need to make tools and simple jewellery. Other merchants will journey south to the ocean, bringing back dried fish, salt and ornamental shells. A merchant who possesses especially valuable goods probably will leave them in the temple for safekeeping when he travels. His belongings are stored in a jar or corded bundle sealed with a lump of clay, on which he has impressed his personal mark with a flat stone disc carved with a ram's head, a bull or some other figure that everyone recognizes as his sign.

Such seals do not represent actual writing, but they are a forerunner; the seals indicate that the Middle Eastern merchants of 4000 B.C. have learned to make signature marks to designate their private property. When the merchant returns from a trip, he reclaims his goods—and naturally makes a present to the gods for keeping them safe.

By 3400 B.C., some six centuries later, the town has grown to a bustling community of 20,000. Its network of villages stretches nearly 15 miles up and down the river. A large part of the expansion has stemmed from an invention of a few generations back: a hoe with a curved handle to which an ox can be hitched. This animal-powered hoe, now in effect a plough, enables the farmer to cultivate much more land, and therefore to produce far more food than his hoe-wielding great-grandfather was able to produce.

Another new invention has appeared, and that is the wheel. Now to carry their big harvests to the town market, the more prosperous farmers are beginning to harness oxen to two-wheeled carts, which are much more efficient as transport than the sledges of their fathers' time.

The market has, of course, expanded to handle the richer crops and it also offers a great variety of goods: timber and limestone, rafted downstream to add to the temple building, and, for the affluent, ornaments of imported silver, carnelian and lapis lazuli. Perhaps the most significant import is copper, brought down in rough ingots from the mountain country some hundreds of miles away, then cast and forged by the town smiths into sickles and knife blades. The new tools —which, like the plough and the wheel, enable the farmers to farm more efficiently than they did before

Excavating and Preserving Words on Clay

As life in ancient Mesopotamia grew increasingly complicated, necessitating the maintenance of more and more records inscribed on tablets of clay, the most important documents were baked hard to preserve them. Tablets that were not kiln-fired frequently disintegrated when handled.

Today's archaeologists have established a standard method to ensure the conservation of such delicate, informative finds. The steps are outlined in the pictures on these pages, photographed at a dig in Iraq.

To these basic procedures, each expert adds his own refinements, often resorting to unexpected tools. One archaeologist uses fine dental probes to remove compacted earth from the inscribed characters. To complete his kit, he carries a grapefruit knife to free the tablets from the ground, and artists' brushes to clean them.

Perhaps the most critical sequence in the technique is the baking and cooling of the tablets, which have to be done slowly lest the fragments become dangerously brittle. Kilns made of local mud bricks and mud plaster may be installed right at the excavation site, or thermostatically controlled ovens off the site can be used.

After firing and cleaning, a rubber mould is made, from which an unlimited number of plaster casts may be prepared to be distributed to scholars anywhere in the world.

After carefully loosening the find from the surrounding earth with a knife, a worker at a dig at Nippur, site of a Sumerian city, uses a paintbrush to remove dirt from the unbaked tablet.

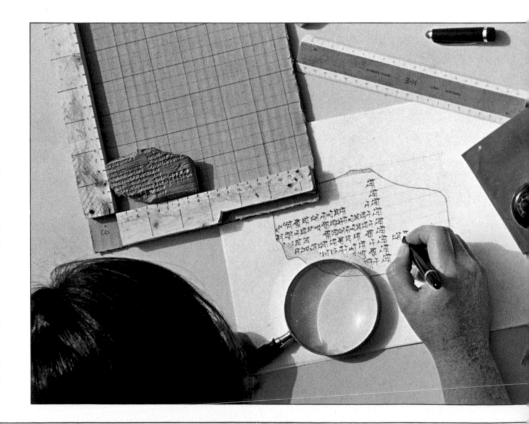

An expert plots the location of the find —information that will aid in dating the tablet—on a grid plan of the area.

An archaeologist puts the tablet in a dish and covers the clay with a layer of sand before baking it in a kiln.

After two days' cooling, the tablet is gently sandblasted to remove salts and bits of earth that may still cling to it.

An epigrapher skilled at copying and reading cuneiform draws the signs in a scale large enough to read easily. Reproducing them on a grid makes it possible to preserve the relationships between the sizes of the original characters and the lengths of the lines.

A member of the field staff lifts from the tablet a finished latex rubber mould into which plaster will be poured to make casts. The casts can be transported to distant museums and universities, while the original must often remain in the country where it was found to comply with regulations against the export of archaeological treasures.

How the Earliest Form of Writing Developed

The first words in writing were pictographs like the figures in the second column of the chart at right. The Sumerians of the Fourth Millennium B.C. scratched these stylized drawings on to clay tablets that fit into the palm of the hand. As tablets increased in size to record ever more information, the scribes found writing easier if the tablets —and the symbols—were turned sideways. At the new angle (*third column*), also adopted by Babylonian and Assyrian scribes, writing that had formerly run in vertical columns set down from right to left now ran horizontally from left to right.

Because a pointed reed raised ridges and bumps in the clay as it was drawn across the soft surface, scribes began to use a blunter instrument that could simply be pressed on the tablet. The resulting wedge-shaped impressions (*fourth column*) kept some resemblance to the original pictograph. But by the middle of the Second Millennium B.C. lingering attempts to maintain realism had yielded to more efficient systems of abstract symbols (*last column*).

Over a period of 2,400 years, Middle Eastern scribes refined the pictorial images of Sumerian times into intricate, abstract cuneiform figures that hardly suggest the actual subjects they originally represented.

Original or derived meaning	Original pictograph	Pictograph in modified position	Early Babylonian	Assyrian
BIRD				
FISH				
OX				
SUN/DAY				
GRAIN				
ORCHARD				

—represent social changes; their manufacture requires specialized craftsmen, and therefore indicates a splintering and multiplication of occupations and professional interests.

The temple has changed no less than the market. After a series of rebuildings, it now stands some 20 feet high above its 30-foot earthen foundation; its walls are decorated with frescoes. The priests and their assistants now number more than 40, and, very significantly, only a few of these are engaged in strictly religious pursuits. The enlarged and beautified temple is more than an incidental by-product of the community's growth in population and wealth; the building also reflects the temple's pre-eminence in the community: by now it owns nearly a tenth of the town and village croplands. Bit by bit, over the centuries, the temple has picked up fields here and there from unlucky or unskilled farmers unable to repay their loans of seed. Once in a while the temple acquires an entire farm, given by a pious elder who

seeks to increase his store of credit with the gods.

Some of the temple lands are worked by sharecropping tenants, the rest by slaves—descendants of unfortunate temple debtors who were forced into servitude to discharge their obligations to the gods, or the offspring of parents who were too poor to feed their large families and therefore dedicated their children to the temple.

The labourers must, of course, be supervised by an overseer in each village where the temple has lands. The overseer also dispenses their rations of bread, beer, beans, a handful of dates—and on feast days a little meat. And since the overseer is responsible to the gods—and their earthly representatives—for the goods he gives out, he keeps records that will be stored in the temple archives.

By the end of the Fourth Millennium B.C., true writing has made its appearance. The technique has advanced beyond the marks stamped on clay by flat seals to identify a merchant's goods. The overseers'

The commonly used word for "orchard" appears circled in each of the tablets below. Comparing the symbol as it appears on the tablets (from left to right) with the chart opposite, the word evolves from a pictured stand of trees in the original Sumerian to a complex combination of wedges in the Assyrian cuneiform.

Early pictograph, 3000 B.C.   Cuneiform, 2500 B.C.   Early Babylonian, 1750 B.C.   Assyrian, 683 B.C.

reports can differentiate among kinds of goods (distinguishing, say, barley grain from beer and meat) as well as indicate the ownership of property and enumerate quantities.

The writing method of the overseer is nevertheless quite simple. From the bed of an irrigation ditch he scoops a handful of mushy clay, lets it partially solidify in a shady place, and shapes and smooths it into a flattish lump measuring perhaps three by five inches—about the size of a modern index card. From a clump of vegetation beside the ditch he cuts a short length of reed and, using his flint knife, sharpens one end of the reed to a point. With this stylus he inscribes pictures on the clay: barley stalks, beer jugs, workers' names. These earliest tablets are as informally put together as the jotted notes a person makes as reminders to himself—and as difficult for somebody else to make out.

But as the tablets come to be more and more widely used, the writers begin to establish conventional signs that always—or nearly always—mean the same thing. Simultaneously, the names of the workers and the commodity inventories begin to be organized in distinct groupings.

As these advances take place, towards the end of the Fourth Millennium, the tablets convey information to readers other than the original writer. At harvest time the overseer sends his written tablets back to the temple, giving the totals of grain, wool and other products that he has loaded into the temple carts. The drivers know that should they pilfer some of their cargo the lading will no longer tally with the tablet, and they can expect a severe flogging. They cannot substitute a counterfeit tablet to conceal their misdeeds; the overseer's tablet is validated with his personal seal—now no longer a flat disc but an engraved cylinder, which repeats its unique pattern on the tablet as it is rolled across the damp clay surface.

The same kind of picture-covered tablet enables

the town priests to keep centralized accounts of the temple's accumulating wealth. The priests have now learned to add up the goods listed on incoming tablets, to subtract goods given out in response to the overseers' requisition tablets and to inventory commodities and other property in stock.

Over the next 200 years writing techniques evolve further. The tablets grow larger: by 2800 B.C. they may measure as much as six by six inches, big enough to hold more than 100 lines. At that size the tablet can no longer be held conveniently in the palm of the hand but must be laid across the forearm. Holding the tablet differently, the scribes find it more comfortable to change the direction of their writing. Instead of proceeding in vertical columns from top to bottom and right to left, they now write in horizontal lines that read from left to right. What has happened is that the columns have been turned anticlockwise, 90 degrees to the left—and with them the symbols have also taken a turn. Now the profiled head that means "head" no longer faces to the right, but gazes upwards.

As the priests develop writing to suit their own ends, they find it expedient to lend their skills to another group within the society: full-time warriors, a new class whose affairs are complex enough to require the keeping of records. The temple's decision to share its precious monopoly on literacy pinpoints an important change in the community power structure. By the time the army begins to use writing, it has become so important—and acquired so much civil authority—that the temple, although continuing to grow in wealth, is forced increasingly to cede to the soldiers some of its once-paramount political influence.

The head of the army, known by the title of *ensi* —meaning "governor" or "protector"—is now also referred to as *lugal*—"big man" or "boss". As head of the town council of elders, outranking the priests, his status in the community is supreme.

In this period the army is manned by the sons of the poorer villagers, who serve between farming chores. The officers are the *lugal*'s close attendants —descendants of mountain tribesmen who in earlier centuries used to harass the lowland villages. One local band has been more ambitious and more shrewd than most. A few generations ago, by playing on mistrust and conflict between rich and poor and between the town and its satellite villages, the band succeeded, with the co-operation of the priests and the richer citizens, in transplanting itself into the town as a force established to keep order. In the course of a few decades, the original band has grown into a professional military aristocracy.

Besides acting as an internal police force, the army has gradually enlarged its ranks to provide the muscle necessary to defend local interests in external disputes. From time to time, in arguments over water and grazing rights, villages on the outlying edges of the town's influence come into conflict with neighbours who are allied with other towns up the river. Such arguments have become increasingly common as the village clusters have multiplied and the wasteland between them has dwindled through burgeoning cultivation. Expanding to meet successive emergencies, the army, which has never demobilized, conducts raids against other towns; from time to time, the force even attacks the tribes in the mountains from which their officers originally came.

An army, of course, must be fed. The officers, who

An unusual document recording a father's pledge of his son's labour as interest on a cash loan is impressed in cuneiform on the upper part of a 3,500-year-old clay tablet from the Mesopotamian city of Nuzi. The contract stipulates that the son is to work for the creditor until either father or son has repaid the principal. The transaction was made legally binding by rolling three seals along the lower part of the tablet; the last seal was that of the scribe.

have now become the aristocrats, still live off the lands that were seized by their tribal ancestors, but the rations of the rank and file are provided through regular contributions from each village. The payments are recorded on clay tablets, kept by apprentice priests provided on loan by the temple.

By 2600 B.C. the community has grown from a town into a city, with a population exceeding 50,000. No longer merely a commercial centre—thanks to the military activities of a succession of expansionist governors—it is now a political centre that dominates the countryside for 50 miles up and down the river, controlling half a dozen clusters of villages, each of which is centred on its own market town. The ruler, or *lugal*, of this complex now has rank equivalent to that of a king. The *ensis*, or governors, of the outlying towns and village complexes have become his direct subordinates.

The city temple is now an ornate structure 30 feet high, set on a terraced mound looming up some 50 feet above the city and visible for miles across the plains. The exterior walls are decorated with geometric patterns made up of thousands of baked pottery cones in black, red and yellow. Its pillars consist of palm logs that glisten with bits of mother-of-pearl set in a matrix of asphalt.

This impressive structure is merely the centrepiece of the city's bustling religious quarter, an enclosure several hundred yards across. The temple complex is almost a city in miniature. It has its own pottery works, carpentry shop, stone-cutter's workshop and warehouses. In the bakery, brewery and kitchen, men prepare the divine repasts ceremonially set before the images of the gods, as well as the somewhat less elaborate meals of the priests and the far simpler fare for the temple slaves and servants.

So essential has writing now become to the conduct of affairs that the temple retains a staff of scribes whose sole duty is to record its operations, which they now do in a script made up of hundreds of ideographic symbols.

The forms of the signs themselves are subtly changing. The scribes, becoming more facile as they face steadily increasing work, have found that a symbol can be most easily made on clay by poking, not scratching. No longer do they trim the reed stylus to a sharp point; now they shave it to a beaded edge, with which they can draw a series of short lines. By 2500 B.C. the incised signs—which no longer look pictorial—are made up of groups of wedges left by the edge of the stylus.

But the temple scribes have relinquished sole possession of the power that goes with literacy; now the civil and military authorities maintain their own scribes to record government decrees on clay tablets. The *lugal* has stopped supervising his *ensi* subordinates—as his predecessors did—by periodic trips around the satellite towns for verbal reports on the state of the government. By 2300 B.C. he has discovered the convenience of dictating a letter of instructions to his scribe, or secretary, who will send the tablet by messenger to the *lugal*'s subordinate. The message will be read out loud to the *ensi* by his own scribe, who will then write down the reply.

Writing has spread to the market-place, where a few merchants are beginning to use the clay tablets to keep track of their prospering enterprises, serving ever more customers over an ever-increasing radius; accounts kept by memory alone can too easily become garbled. The city's trade network now extends for hundreds of miles, gathering incense and pearls from the land of Dilmun on the Persian Gulf; copper, tin and silver from the mountains of the distant north; and gold and fine linen from Egypt, the mighty kingdom that rules another great river plain that lies a thousand miles to the west.

Commodities from farthest away are obtained through a series of middlemen, each of them moving the goods a few hundred miles and then bartering them to the next merchant down the line. To conduct these transactions, and those closer to home, the merchant increasingly finds himself dictating letters to a public letter writer for forwarding to correspondents in other cities: ordering copper ingots, baskets of dates, or pots containing clay, and indicating to the potential customer an offering price, quoted in weight units of silver or copper.

As a result of this activity, the public letter writer has become an institution. In addition to writing business letters, he may occasionally inscribe a personal message for some ordinary citizen. In time, however, the bulk of his work will concern land transactions, a highly complicated scribal speciality. It used to be that everyone knew who owned which fields, but now, across the several hundred square miles of territory ruled by the city, the holdings of some wealthy landowners may be scattered among half a dozen different towns and villages, and it is hard to keep track of who owns what.

If land taxes are to be justly assessed by the *lugal*, there must be some permanent record of who owns a given field—a document certifying that in the third year of the reign of King So and So, A, son of B, sold such and such a field to C, son of D, for this or

Text continued on page 74

Inscriptions That Placated Gods and Immortalized Men

For thousands of years, commemorative writing, built into a monument's structure, has served to immortalize men. In ancient times at the dedication of a temple or a palace—as today at the laying of a cornerstone for a town hall—names and dates were indelibly inscribed on a building's foundation. In the Middle East, beginning almost 5,000 years ago, writing placed in buildings served to perpetuate the memory of the builder-ruler and also to win favour with the gods.

By constructing or renovating a building and dedicating it to a deity, a king could hope to preserve himself and his people from evil. To ensure that the protection endured, suitably inscribed nails, clay tablets, bricks and statues were placed in foundations. Sometimes a "time capsule" box was also inserted; it held records describing the monument's construction, from the metals used to the countries supplying materials. As if all that were not enough to assure the benevolence of the gods, a king would include a list of every other pious deed accomplished during his reign.

The headless statue of Gudea, a Sumerian ruler of 2100 B.C., was carved with the tools of an architect on his lap. The writing on his skirt describes a restoration of a temple dedicated to the god Ningirsu. It also places a curse on anyone destroying the inscription.

Objects to Secure Divine Favour

Inscribed dedicatory figures, like the ones below and at right, were embedded in the lower walls of ancient Sumerian buildings as a memorial to the King who commissioned the construction. Once set in place—standing upright with their points touching the ground—they were concealed by successive courses of bricks.

A rich cache of such objects was found during the 1968 excavations of a temple at Lagash, near the modern town of Shatra, in Iraq. In the foundations archaeologists turned up the devotional figures below, placed there in the monarch's behalf to evoke the favour of the gods. The King, believing that many copies increased his chances of divine intercession, took care to install several objects.

Identically inscribed copper figures dating from 2500 B.C. were found in a temple wall. The gist of the message was simple: "Enannatum, Governor of Lagash, has dedicated the temple to Inanna for Enannatum's well-being."

Bearing an inscription of the Sumerian king Gudea, this bronze figure, dating from 2100 B.C., was implanted in the foundation of a building near Lagash. According to some scholars, the nail he is holding was meant to drive out evil.

A trilingual gold plaque of the Sixth Century B.C.—inscribed in Old Persian, Elamite and Babylonian—is one of a pair, each matched by a silver duplicate, placed by Persia's King Darius in the audience hall at Persepolis. The text asks the god Ahuramazda to protect Darius and guard his royal house.

that amount of silver or copper, as attested by the names and personal seals of A and C, and the name of the scribe as witness. Similarly, a peasant or merchant seeking to borrow grain or copper against his land or goods must provide the lender with the security of a written mortgage or promissory note. All these documents have the force of law. If necessary, the mortgage holder can call on the government to enforce his written right to the land or to the goods that have been called into question.

By 2000 B.C. a dozen or more cities much like the imaginary one just sketched made up the Sumerian civilization. Each had grown from a tiny village of related families to a thriving metropolis of diverse peoples with varied occupations. And all the inhabitants, from king to labourers, were directly or indirectly affected by the institution of writing, whether or not they understood its nature or its uses.

As the cities grew more complex, so did the craft of writing. Through 500 years of evolution, it changed in outward appearance and internal structure as well. Beginning with realistic pictures of familiar objects in everyday life—a sheaf of grain, a human head, an ox, a fish, a bird, the sun, a star—and proceeding to associated ideas, such as eating (the grain), speaking (the head), working (the ox) and worshipping (the sun and stars), writing acquired a viable vocabulary of some 2,000 word symbols.

After another half millennium, with repeated usage and more facility on the part of the scribes, the word signs had ceased to be realistic pictures: they had become abstract symbols, including many signs that communicated the sounds of words. The script, set down in characters made of wedge-shaped signs,

Stamping-moulds with rounded handles, like the tool above, were used by Mesopotamian masons to mark bricks used in the building of temples and royal edifices. The face of the stamp shown above commemorates the King who ordered construction of the temple of Enlil at Nippur in 2200 B.C.

was capable of expressing almost any thought that a person might conceive. This cuneiform writing eventually became the most widely used script throughout the ancient world of the Middle East.

Devising signs to represent the sounds of spoken language must have been a challenging task when it came to writing personal proper names—one of the early concepts (along with numbers and labels for such commodities as grain) to require and find written expression. Though a number or a commodity can be represented easily enough in a picture or a series of pictures, names are more complicated. Some Sumerians undoubtedly had descriptive names, like the American Indian's White Buffalo or He-Dog, that were easily pictured. Two fairly common names in early Sumerian accounts are Lulim, shown by the word sign for "deer", and Lul-a, shown by the sign for "fox", almost certainly referring to men named Deer and Fox. An interesting, if unanswerable, question is whether such names were nicknames made up by the priestly accountants. Similar accounting tablets from Mycenaean Crete around 1400 B.C. sometimes list slaves by such epithets as "Scabby" and "Squint".

But such names, whether or not they were sobriquets, were in the minority. A name frequently found in early records is Enlil-ti. It embodies the name of a god—Enlil—and means, approximately, "Oh-Enlil-Give-Life". This approach is not very different in spirit from that of the English Puritans, who gave their children such names as Prudence and Charity or Praise-God and Saved-from-Captivity. The word for "life" in Sumerian is pronounced "ti", as is the word for "arrow". This identity in sound of the two words brings the rebus principle into play. It seems

paradoxical, at first glance, that a picture of an arrow —a deadly weapon—incorporated in an ancient name should represent the concept of life. But languages everywhere have homonyms—words that sound alike but have entirely different meanings. In English the letter T, the golfer's tee and afternoon tea bear no relation to one another, but all sound exactly alike when spoken aloud.

The idea content of names is not the only reason why the Sumerians were impelled to seek a way of picturing sounds. Sumerian was an agglutinative language—defined by linguists as one in which the word roots remain constant, and grammatical variations are indicated by the addition of interchangeable prefixes and suffixes. English, technically not an agglutinative language, has no perfect analogy, but an indication of how the agglutinative principle works can be seen in the words "outstanding", "understanding", "upstanding" and "notwithstanding". Because of the prefixes, all four words convey totally different meanings, yet all four of them rest on a single root: the verb "to stand".

Besides working this kind of change, in Sumerian agglutination was used to decline and to modify nouns, and to conjugate verbs. The noun e, for instance, meant "house"; but a suffix could qualify it so that e-zu meant "house-your". Similarly, the verb gar meant "to put"; gar-ra meant "put" in the past tense; and ha-gar meant "put" in the subjunctive mood, as in "May he put some grain in storage today".

Because Sumerian was rich in one-syllable nouns and verbs, all of them declined and conjugated with prefixes and suffixes, and because many of the syllables overlapped in sound, rebus writing—"eye saw"—arose quite easily. For instance, the Sumerian word *ka* meant "mouth", an idea that was easily pictured. But the same sound also had a genitive meaning, like the ending "-'s" or the pronoun "his", in English. So it was easy to record the idea "the man's house"—in Sumerian *e-lu-ka*—by combining the signs for house, man and mouth (his).

All this seems fairly simple. But in a language full of one-syllable words, the rebus principle could make for ambiguity of meaning: examples in English are "so", "sew" and "sow", distinguishable only in context. The Sumerians dealt with such ambiguities by introducing a written sign to provide such a context: the determinative, a sign placed at the beginning or end of a word to indicate to what class of word it belongs. English has no real determinatives; a sign that closely resembles one is the dollar sign ($), placed before a numeral to show a sum of money in U.S. currency. The Sumerians used many determinatives, extensively and insistently. They put the sign for the word "bird" after the name of any bird, whether a bluebird or hawk. The sign for the word "wood" appeared before the name of any wooden object, whether tree, boat or plough. And when the Sumerians wished to indicate a farmer—that is, a man who lived by wielding a plough—the determinative sign for "man" replaced the one for "wood" in front of the basic sign for "plough".

When Sumerian cuneiform had reached this relatively workable stage, it began to spread abroad, where it was adapted to an astonishing variety of languages that had no connection with Sumerian. As early as 2600 B.C., cuneiform was beginning to be used in central and northern Mesopotamia by the Akkadians, who spoke a Semitic tongue. By the middle of the Third Millennium, cuneiform had spread northeast to Elam, where it replaced the script that was then being used to record the Elamite language. By around 1500 B.C. the script had arrived in Asia Minor, where it was used by Hurrians and Hittites—and much later by Urartians as well.

By the middle of the Second Millennium other scripts would rise along the Mediterranean and overtake cuneiform. But the pioneer script had a long life ahead: as late as A.D. 75 a version was still in use in what is now Iraq.

The spread of cuneiform is easy to explain. The Sumerians traded far and wide, and they crossed paths with all the peoples of the Middle East. But cuneiform would not have become so pervasive had it not been so adaptable—a characteristic that arose from the diversity of language and make-up of the peoples who developed it.

From the start, the inhabitants of Sumer spoke many languages besides Sumerian. In southern Mesopotamia the Sumerian people were dominant in power, and perhaps also in numbers, from 4000 B.C. until about 2000 B.C.; but the cities harboured many non-Sumerians—and their languages.

An important non-Sumerian element was a group of proto-Euphrateans, descendants of the people who are presumed to have inhabited southern Mesopotamia before the Sumerians arrived. The existence of such a people has been deduced in two ways. First, Sumerian mythology suggests that the Sumerians did not themselves originate in Mesopotamia, but came from the mountainous region to the north. Second, many Sumerian geographical names make no more sense as Sumerian words than some American place names make in English. The Potomac and Mis-

TO FOOL THE UNWARY, A PHONY BOWL AND A FRAUDULENT TABLET

The citizens of Nippur, Iraq, bought clay bowls, inscribed with incantations in Aramaic, under which they trapped evil spirits. The bowl at left bears authentic writing; the one at right, painted with meaningless scrawls, was sold to gullible illiterates.

During the last century, hundreds of fake Babylonian clay tablets were sold by a London dealer to U.S. museums. They were not studied for many years, but the recent manufacture of the cast specimen at right became obvious when it came apart at the seam.

sissippi rivers, for instance, were named by American Indian tribes, in whose tongues the words meant "trading place" and "great river" respectively; and the English-speaking newcomers to the land adopted the names given the rivers by the indigenous peoples they found there.

The same thing seems to have happened with place names in Sumer. The rivers today called the Tigris and the Euphrates were known to the Sumerians as the Idigna and the Buranun. To some scholars these names do not suggest Sumerian origin any more than the name Mississippi conveys the idea of an English derivation. There is a logical suspicion that the rivers were named by earlier inhabitants, speaking a quite different tongue.

In addition to the aboriginal non-Sumerians who might have named the region's rivers, the population included a sprinkling of Elamites and other easterners, many mountain women and mountain men brought down as slaves, and mountain people who had settled in the cities on their own. Sumer was also home for speakers of various Semitic tongues and dialects related to Hebrew, Arabic and Aramaic, the language of Christ. By 2000 B.C. certain Semitic words had become common in Sumerian documents —usually the names for such occupations as merchant and smith, and such newly invented devices as the mirror, which the Sumerians had borrowed from Semitic inventors.

As cuneiform passed from Sumerian into other languages, its basic form was retained in logograms, or word signs. In time, as speakers of other languages adapted the signs to the sounds of their own tongues, the signs began to change; and as people made wider and wider use of phonetics, they began to introduce their own syllabic signs to take the place of word signs. As that happened, the number of signs diminished from thousands to hundreds, for the simple reason that the same syllable could stand for increasing numbers of word parts.

But some word signs (and a good many determinatives) survived intact for centuries, through many language changes. The cuneiform sign for "king" is a case in point. The same symbol stood for a word that was spoken *lugal* in Sumerian, *sharru* in Akkadian, *hassus* in Hittite and *ewirne* in Hurrian.

The persistence of word signs and determinatives from one version of cuneiform to another ultimately proved to be of immense help to modern scholars seeking to decipher unknown tongues. When researchers found word signs in undeciphered Sumerian and Hittite that were already familiar from Akkadian inscriptions, meanings could often be worked out even when pronunciation could not. Likewise, the appearance of a familiar determinative, even if it did not identify the precise meaning of the word it accompanied, often indicated what general sort of object was under discussion.

About 2300 B.C., after more than a millennium of preeminence in southern Mesopotamia, the Sumerians succumbed to the Akkadians, a Semitic-speaking people who founded the city of Akkad in the north. Sumer ceased to exist as a loose collection of kindred city-states. The language their peoples had spoken was replaced by Akkadian. The Akkadians had been ascending in political and economic importance since the middle of the Third Millennium; in the Second Millennium, after swallowing up the Sumerian people, they were to beget the Babylonian Empire. Yet Sumerian culture was far from dead. For among the Sumerian legacies to the ancient Middle East—one that made its appearance almost as early as writing itself—was the school; through that medium Sumerian civilization was to be transmitted to generations of Mesopotamian schoolboys.

Varied Roles of the Scribal Elite

In the bustling world of Babylonia some 4,000 years ago, the professional scribe had already become indispensable. Manipulating his stylus of wood or reed with the speed of a knitting needle, he created the records that made possible a sophisticated civilization and bound it together.

Through the medium of the scribe's skills, a king sent instructions to his far-flung administrators, his collectors kept tax accounts, merchants among his subjects ordered goods and billed customers, and the more prosperous farmers bought and sold land.

Obviously, any man who could write enjoyed high regard. But the profession, like most callings, was divided into many levels and specialities. Ranking lowest was the scribe of the market-place: for a fee, he turned out business correspondence and personal letters. At the highest level, a scribe who grasped the intricacies of mathematics was likely to be among the most important men in his community; some, indeed, rose to become counsellors to kings.

In a market-place a scribe, watched by his son, takes dictation from a merchant (foreground). Using a short reed stylus held in his right hand, the writer transforms the spoken words into symbols impressed on a clay tablet in his left palm. The pot near the scribe contains a supply of wet clay.

The Schooling of a Scribe

From early morning to late afternoon, for 24 days in every 30, from age six to 18—that was the study regimen for a Babylonian schoolboy who aspired to become a scribe.

In this hard academy, a boy endured ceaseless drilling under the guidance of a headmaster and a staff of assistants, including a monitor who was specifically assigned to beat him whenever he made a mistake. The drills led to proficiency in writing both Akkadian—the Babylonian tongue—and Sumerian, the classical language. Among other required subjects were mathematics, literature and the preparation of legal contracts.

No wonder that long before the stiff examination that ended the ordeal of school, many a student had dropped out—or flunked. The best that such an outcast could expect for all his trouble was a humble post as a village letter writer.

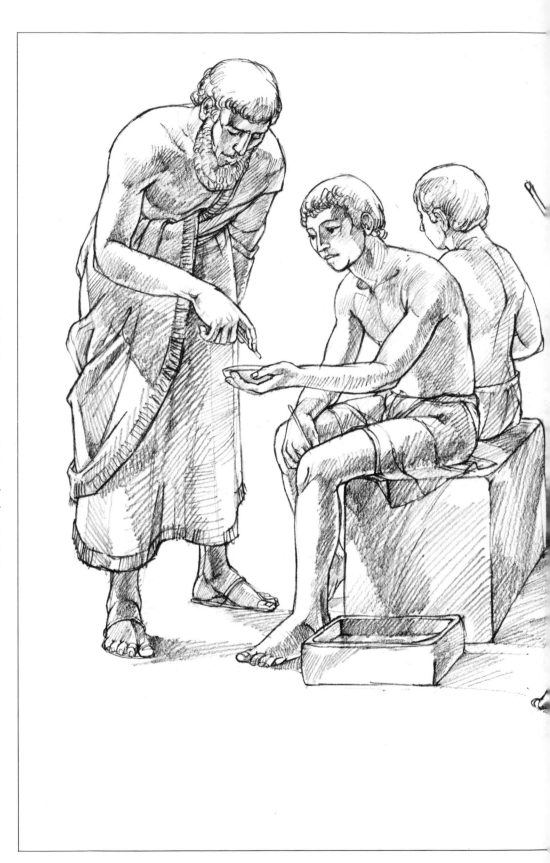

Sitting on plastered brick benches in a Middle Eastern classroom of 1800 B.C., schoolboys are put through their paces. At left, the head teacher is about to demonstrate the proper execution of a word sign; at rear, holding a rod, an assistant teacher notes poor work by a would-be scribe who may be caned as punishment. In the foreground, a student takes clay from a pot for a fresh tablet; to his left, a boy moistens his tablet in a water pan. Standing beside the last bench, an apprentice teacher coaches a young student.

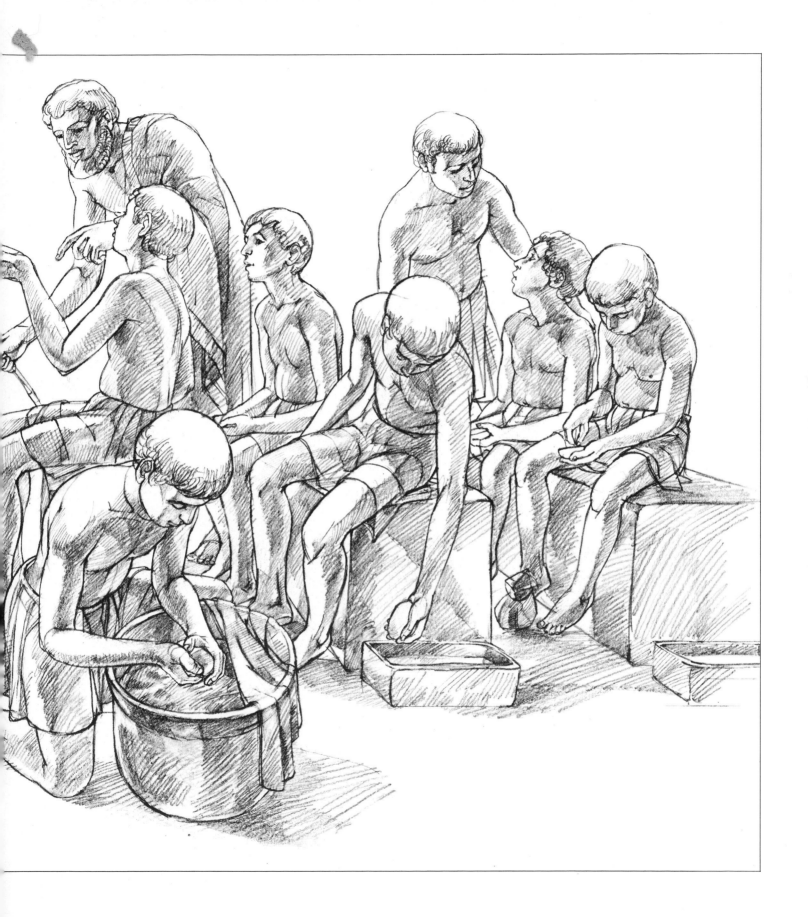

Keepers of Contracts and Accounts

Graduates of a school for scribes had no trouble keeping busy. The civilization in which Babylonia flourished was dedicated to the rule of law: virtually no transaction, however small, was legal unless it was formally recorded in writing.

A scribe could thus earn a good living as a notary public, like the man in the foreground at near right. The basic job was preparing contracts for sales of real estate or other property. The terms of the deal were often set down on two identical clay tablets, signed with the personal seals of the contracting parties, the scribe and two witnesses. The terms were repeated on the two identical clay envelopes in which the tablets were then encased. Only in the event of a lawsuit were the envelopes broken and the original tablets offered as evidence of the contract's terms.

Scribes who preferred steady employment to the ups and downs of independent practice found jobs easily —as, say, keepers of accounts for shippers and merchants or as members of the temple staff, issuing receipts to the pious for offerings.

In his office, a scribe crimps closed an envelope around one copy of a land sale contract. Observed by two witnesses (standing), the first party to the deal, seated at the desk, runs his seal over the other copy while the second party watches him attentively.

A scribe employed by the bearded merchant (above, left) jots down the tally for a cargo just arrived from the south by canal boat that is now in the process of being unloaded. The freight ordered by the merchant consists of rolls of reed mats to be used for roofing and for carpeting; there are also square bales of sheepskins that are to be sold to tanners. In the water at the edge of the canal is a gufa, a circular basket-weave craft that is used to ferry passengers across the canal.

A temple scribe (third from left), seated in a courtyard just outside the temple walls, writes clay memoranda recording the offerings of goats, geese, baskets of fish and dates, and the names of the donors. At the week's end, he will transfer the information to a ledger—a larger clay tablet—where he keeps the temple accounts. A fellow scribe (seated, left) issues receipts for the offerings so that the givers can prove to the temple officials they have fulfilled their religious obligations.

The Surveyor: A Man of Complex Skills

Among the most demanding aspects of the scribe's profession was the surveying of land. As is still true, the procedure was essential for the sale of real estate as well as for the assessment of taxes, the settlement of wills bequeathing property to be divided among a number of heirs and the adjudication of inevitable disputes between neighbours.

But only the best educated and brightest of scribes, such as the man standing in the right foreground, were equal to the complex mathematical calculations that surveying required. Most fields were irregular in shape, and the sole measuring device known to have been available was a rope divided by equidistant markings. Yet surveyor-scribes, using a sophisticated system of numerical notation long before the Greeks developed geometry, could determine accurately the area of any piece of land, however peculiar its shape.

A man who possessed the brains and the background for surveying could—if he was truly fortunate—rise to become the head of the bureaucracy that ran the country.

While assistants using a knotted rope carefully measure a canal-side field of barley, the master surveyor (standing, right) notes on clay the figures that they call out; he will make his calculations later. To his right, another assistant prepares more tablets.

In the Babylonian city of Nippur, about 1800 B.C., 12-year-old Sinmagir is on his way to school. Only half an hour ago he lay curled beneath a blanket in the little mud-brick room he shares with his younger sister. Then, as the long shadows of dawn struck across the Mesopotamian countryside east of the city, his mother gently shook him awake. Throwing a light wool tunic over his linen loincloth, he stepped into the house courtyard to splash his face with water brought from the near-by canal. In the kitchen, his mother handed him a bowl of barley porridge, whose warmth was pleasant in the chill of early morning. Breakfast over, she gave him his leather satchel containing his reed stylus, his homework—a clay tablet whose inscriptions he had to memorize—and his lunch: two flattened rolls of soft bread slit and filled with bits of meat and onion, and a handful of dates. Then, with a brief embrace, she sent him off.

Now, trotting through the narrow alley called the Street of the Goldsmiths, where his father is a prosperous merchant, Sinmagir makes his way towards the market-place. The bustle of dawn is already rising to a concerto of gossip, argument, donkey drivers' shouts and hawkers' cries. The square is filled with things to tempt a boy's eye and curiosity: stalls selling skewers of broiled mutton and sweetmeats of nuts and honey; a small tavern where a few teamsters are having their first beer of the day; craftsmen crying their wares of leather, bronze and pottery; a

In this 12th Century B.C. tomb painting, the Egyptian god Thoth, patron of scribes and the mythical inventor of writing, appears in the guise of a baboon—an animal sacred to the city of Hermopolis. In his right hand he holds a scribe's palette; with his left he reaches towards the prow of a boat belonging to the powerful Sun God, whose companion he was.

knot of fierce Hurrian mountaineers staring about at the sights of the city; a public letter writer working to get the lumps out of a potful of clay that he will shape into flat tablets to take down the day's writing. But despite the distractions, Sinmagir presses on; lateness—as the cane wielded by the monitor, the school disciplinarian, reminded him only last week—is severely punished.

Arriving at the school gate, he greets his classmates and then nods politely to the gatekeeper—a tough, one-eyed ex-soldier whose long arm and short temper encourage the boys to keep on his good side. Amid a certain amount of scuffling, Sinmagir takes his place on one of the classroom benches. The headmaster, who is called the school father, enters the room; the 30-odd boys rise and bow to him ceremoniously, and the day's work begins.

First each boy must recite his homework. For the littlest ones, this recitation is a list of syllables. "Tu, ta, ti; bu, ba, bi," they chant, reciting the names of the syllables used to write Akkadian, the language they speak, as modern children might recite the letters of the alphabet. At his age, however, Sinmagir has long since done with such elementary exercises; his own assignment is a list of words naming the parts of the human body. He has written the wedge-shaped signs on his clay tablet and now must read aloud. Though he stumbles once or twice, he receives no more than a hard look from the school father, but one of his friends is not so lucky. The boy has obviously not studied at all, and makes a hash of his recitation. He is sentenced to three strokes of the cane, which the monitor deals out then and there.

The headmaster now withdraws to another room, where he will work with a group of advanced students, and three assistant teachers take over the class. These are older boys, whom Sinmagir and his classmates ceremoniously address as "elder brothers", and who are entitled to employ the cane on inattentive or unruly juniors. Each boy is called to the front of the room, where he is given a chunk of moist clay from a pot covered with a wet cloth. Returning to their desks, the pupils knead the clay smooth, pressing out bubbles and picking out bits of grit and straw, and shape the lumps into the bun-shaped slabs that are their equivalent of exercise books. A few students on the back benches pinch off pellets of clay, which they surreptitiously flick at their fellows. The elder brothers then pass along the rows, inscribing on the left side of each tablet a new list of words that Sinmagir and his fellows must copy. By the time the work is done and the copies are inspected and corrected, it is time for lunch.

During the lunchtime recess, a few energetic boys start a game of tag, but with the midday sun beating down into the school courtyard most are content with quieter recreations such as knucklebones, a remote ancestor of jacks.

After lunch comes arithmetic. The little boys recite in unison the tables of longitudinal measurement: "30 *ubanu* make one *ammatu*, six *ammatu* make one *ganû*, two *ganû* make one *ashlu*," they say. They also commit to memory measures of area, volume and weight. But Sinmagir is past that. He and the others of his age are put to problems in addition and subtraction, using examples taken from everyday life. The basic unit of weight measurement is the talent, which is divided into 60 minas, each weighing about one pound. A problem might read: what is the total weight of three baskets containing 30, 45 and 75 minas of wheat? Or if a farmer has five talents of wheat and pays his workers with 40 minas of it, how much does he have left?

In another year, these boys will be ready for multiplication and division. The problems, in this case, may involve the areas of fields, figured by multiplying the linear measurements for length and width in *gar* (equivalent to 20 feet) and totalled in *iku* (37,600 square feet). What is the area of a field five *gar* by seven? How does a scribe divide a field of six *iku* among a farmer's three sons so that the eldest receives twice as much as the other two?

By midafternoon it is time for the lesson in Sumerian, the language of the venerable civilization that is the ancestor of their own. In the time of Sinmagir and his classmates, though some of their fathers boast of having Sumerian blood and a few even bear Sumerian names, the language itself is no longer spoken except in the schools and in the temples. But the Babylonians look to the Sumerians as their cultural forbears; and, as the headmaster is fond of reminding the boys, no man can call himself educated unless he can read and write the ancient script.

For that purpose the tablets are scraped clean of earlier lessons and the instructor dictates in Sumerian a list of easy Akkadian words that the boys already know how to write. These they put in a column, one word below the other, and the instructor then passes around tablets listing the Sumerian equivalents, which the boys then copy on to their own tablets. In another year, Sinmagir and his classmates will proceed to Sumerian grammar, and eventually they will be able to write short sentences and stories in the ancient tongue.

At last it is time to copy down the assignment for

An exercise for a Babylonian seven-year-old on his first day at school was mastering the elementary sign for "dish" by impressing it again and again on both sides of a clay tablet. This sample, from Nippur, dates from about 1700 B.C.

In this tablet, dating from 2600 B.C., a Sumerian schoolboy has shown that he had much to learn: his wedges are not even; he has left out details in the sign for "king" (top arrow), and has turned the sign for "dust" (bottom arrow) on its side. Accurate renditions of the signs are drawn outside the tablet.

the next day. Then the boys burst forth from the classroom into the sloping sunlight of late afternoon, crowd through the gate and race towards home, yelling like demons at their release from bondage. At home Sinmagir will have his supper, and before ending his day he will recite his homework to his admiring parents, who, though members of the upper middle class, are illiterate.

Such was the instruction offered in a Mesopotamian school at the beginning of the Second Millennium B.C. Several sites have yielded thousands of clay tablets—some 30,000 turned up in the city of Nippur alone—showing texts to be learned, exercises done in childish hands and some essays describing the life the students led. The preceding account is pieced together from several such tablets, originating at a number of sites.

The student who graduated from a scribal school entered a professional class that constituted a quasi-aristocracy, for very few people could read or write. But inasmuch as the cities of Mesopotamia came very early to rely on written documents for the conduct of business, the promulgation of laws, the settling of contracts and the preservation of religious lore, the scribe was a pivotal figure in his society. He was the link between the king and his subjects, the temple and its faithful, the merchant and his customers, and between the ancient ways and young minds. He was the repository of the lore of his people, the conveyor of the laws of the land, the witness to contracts. For all these reasons, writing was a route to social distinction, political power, intellectual excitement and personal prosperity.

Schools in the ancient world of Mesopotamia—and

also of Egypt, the other site of early writing in the Middle East—arose about 3000 B.C., almost as soon as writing itself began. Almost from its inception, writing was set apart from other trades and occupations. The distinction—a critical one—was based on the relative difficulty of learning. The skills of the master smith and the potter, the craft of the merchant and the ship's captain, intricate and difficult though they were, could always be acquired by watching and doing; they were passed from father to son or from master to apprentice, the novice working as an assistant to the expert. Indeed, nearly all these occupations involved a host of physical skills that could be learned *only* by doing. Anyone who has acquired the trick of making a pot that will withstand firing, or of steering a boat under varying conditions of wind and wave, knows well enough that in such endeavours experience counts for much more towards the learning process than book knowledge.

Learning to write was altogether different. The physical skills involved—in Mesopotamia managing a stylus of reed or wood on clay, and in Egypt wielding an inked brush on papyrus—were modest, but the mental skills required were enormous. Writing demanded that hundreds of complicated signs be memorized. The standard grammar of ancient Egyptian, compiled in the 1920s by the eminent English Egyptologist Sir Alan Gardiner, lists more than 700 hieroglyphs—and the list of Mesopotamian cuneiform symbols was no shorter. The meanings of the signs were mostly arbitrary, and therefore they were difficult to learn by heart. Finally, the rules for combining the signs with one another introduced yet other complexities: the whole apparatus of word signs, syllabic signs and determinatives.

This fragment of a 3,700-year-old Babylonian tablet includes geometry exercises that student scribes had to perform in the process of learning to read and write. The dimensions of the various squares are recorded in the cuneiform texts under each example, suggesting that the pupils were to calculate the areas of the rectangles, triangles and circles inside them.

To commit all this material to memory required up to a dozen years of concentrated effort. And during virtually all that time the novice scribe, unlike novices in other crafts, would be wholly worthless to his teacher. The apprentice smith, though he lacked the skill to cast a bronze axehead or temper a dagger, could still help his master by gathering fuel for the forge, manning the bellows or holding the work steady with pincers on the stone anvil. Little by little, he could take over such jobs as hammering out nails and hoe blades. But there were no comparably simple tasks at hand for an apprentice scribe. The physical act of writing was—and still is—a one-man operation. An unskilled assistant is more hindrance than help.

In the early days of writing, professional scribes may well have passed their demanding craft on to their sons—and occasionally their daughters, for the names of a few female scribes crop up in ancient documents. But any other youngster seeking to learn the scribe's trade would find no one interested in taking him on as an assistant—unless he or his parents paid the instructor for the time and trouble. And that sort of relationship, in which A is paid to convey information and skills to B, is the school in embryo. For the first scribes who gave private lessons, it could hardly have taken very long to make the discovery that they could multiply their incomes by teaching students in groups rather than one at a time. Almost as soon, other scribes must have realized that it was far simpler to send their own sons off to school than it was to teach them at home.

In Egypt, where the Pharaoh was god and where religious and state affairs were closely intertwined, education seems to have begun as a temple monopoly and remained so for many centuries. In Mesopotamia it is not unlikely that the first schools were attached to the temples in which so many scribes worked. But civil rule became distinct from temple affairs at an early date, and private schools of the type the fictitious Sinmagir attended were in existence by 2000 B.C. at the latest; the school father and his assistants offered learning to the community in much the same way that the butcher supplied meat and the farmer provided grain.

Students at the scribe schools were drawn almost entirely from one class of people. Studies of documents from the centuries just after 2000 B.C. show that of some 500 Mesopotamian scribes who kept records of their genealogy, the vast majority came from society's middle ranks: they were usually the sons of sea captains, merchants, accountants, managers or foremen, as well as what in modern times are called civil servants, ranging in positions all the way from ambassador to scribe and archivist.

Some of the less affluent parents from this class doubtless scrimped to give their sons an education, as some still do, but for the sons of the poor, literacy was far out of reach. The peasants and city labourers who made up the great mass of the population could not afford either the cost of tuition or the time lost in class by the student; if the family was to survive, its sons had to be put to work in the fields or some other gainful occupation from childhood on. At the other end of the social scale, the aristocrats seem to have spent a good deal of their time in such gentlemanly pursuits as hunting, warfare and conspicuous consumption —as aristocrats continued to do for thousands of years thereafter. Most of them seem to have been as illiterate as the humblest peasant.

The middle-class boy in Mesopotamia whose family wished him to become a *dubsar*, or tablet writer, would enter the *edubba*, the tablet house, at an early age—probably when he was no more than five or six. He would remain at school, as some clay tablet accounts vaguely put it, "from childhood to manhood," which perhaps meant for 10 or 12 years—that is, until he was 16 or 18 years old.

The process of elementary education consumed as much time in the Middle East at this period as learning to read and write Chinese does today; to master the Chinese language—a system of writing comparable to cuneiform in its complex combination of word signs, phonetic signs and determinatives—takes the average youngster in China about 10 years.

In the ancient Middle Eastern schools, the method of learning seems to have consisted largely of memorizing by rote long written lists of words, usually grouped by subject: parts of the body, trees and wooden objects of all sorts, other plants and animals Later, the students were required to memorize and write down whole documents—hymns, legends, essays, model letters and the like.

The schoolmaster's main educational tool seems to have been the cane. One clay tablet found in Nippur —a 90-line essay that was given the title "Schooldays" by Samuel Noah Kramer, who translated it in the 1940s—describes how a boy could be beaten for not doing his homework, for loitering in the street, for lateness, for speaking without permission, for writing sloppily and for various other offences whose precise nature cannot yet be determined from the tablet. But there is no question about the nature of the chastisement: the word that indicates the punishment combines the Sumerian signs for "stick" and "flesh".

The narrator of "Schooldays" declares: "I began to hate the scribal art, began to neglect the scribal art".

If schooldays in Mesopotamia were frequently painful for the students, they were always arduous; classes began shortly after sunrise and ended not long before sunset—an average of perhaps 11 hours a day. The boys had six days off each month, only three of which were free days. The other three were holy days, and on those days attendance at religious festivals was probably obligatory for teachers and students alike.

The students' busy schedule allowed time for a variety of subjects. Surviving documents reveal that the staff of the typical school usually included, in addition to the school father, the elder brothers, "the man in charge of the whip" and several specialized teachers such as "the man in charge of drawing".

It is not clear just what the course in drawing involved, apart from the likelihood that it did not concern the fine arts, which in the ancient world were the concern of artisans, not scribes. Rather, the drawing class in the *edubba* probably combined elements of what would today be called surveying and architecture—the drawing of maps and plans for the construction of public buildings. A map of Nippur made about 1500 B.C. depicts the city walls, the elaborate canal system that surrounded them, and the docks and the principal buildings, all of which are carefully labelled. The map's accuracy seems to have been confirmed by modern excavations.

But if the curriculum had no fine arts, it did include some of what would today be called liberal arts: the students learned to sing and to conduct a choir, and to use various musical instruments, including flutes, harps and lutes (*page 144*).

Text continued on page 97

The Valued Implements of a Writer

The scribes of Egypt drew a marked distinction between the trades of such labourers as metalsmiths or stonemasons and their own more intellectual profession. But like all artisans, the scribes took great pride in the tools and materials of their craft, shown on this and the following pages. Indeed, the word for "scribe" in hieroglyphic writing combined pictures of the writers' implements —ink palette, water jug and brushes—with the pictograph of a man. When one prominent scribe had his portrait made (*below*) during the Third Millennium B.C., he instructed the sculptor to include his professional gear, which he clearly viewed as a badge of prestige.

In the 4,700-year-old wood carving at the right, Hesire, chief of the royal Egyptian scribes, carries his tools slung over his right shoulder. The writing kit, reconstructed above, included, from right to left, a slate palette with two depressions for holding ink cakes, a wood case to hold a rush brush and a jug for water with which to moisten the brush. The three elements were tied together with twine of flax fibres.

Papyrus Reeds—a Hardy Writing Material

When aspiring Egyptian scribes started their 10 to 12 years of formal education, they were outfitted with inks made from soot, rush brushes and wooden or stone slabs on which to practice. Not until they developed proficiency in executing the 700 hieroglyphs they had to memorize could they begin writing on papyrus. It was not true paper, which is manufactured today from rag or wood pulp, but was made from the fibrous stalks of papyrus reeds (*right*). After the reeds were harvested (*below*), cuttings from the fibres were processed to form coarse, textured sheets (*opposite*).

Papyrus (left), a swamp reed whose name is the source of the word "paper", once grew thickly in the Nile Valley. But the plant's watery habitat has shrunk, and papyrus is found today only in a few private and botanical gardens.

Under the eyes of herons, workers harvest papyrus reeds in this 4,500-year-old stone bas-relief from a tomb at Sakkarah. As the labourer on the left pulls the plants up by the roots, other men carry away bundles of reeds to be made into papyrus sheets and other products such as ropes and baskets. The roots of the plant were considered a great table delicacy by the ancient Egyptians. So abundant was papyrus in northern Egypt until the Middle Ages that it became an emblem for the area.

A section from a 13th Century B.C. funerary text written down on papyrus shows Thoth, a divine patron of scribes, carrying the traditional palette, jug and brushes. This fragment clearly reveals the texture of the papyrus. Made from thin, longitudinal sections of the plant's fibrous stem, each finished sheet actually consisted of two layers that were placed at right angles to each other, then pounded with stones until they fused. This process resulted in a crosshatched effect.

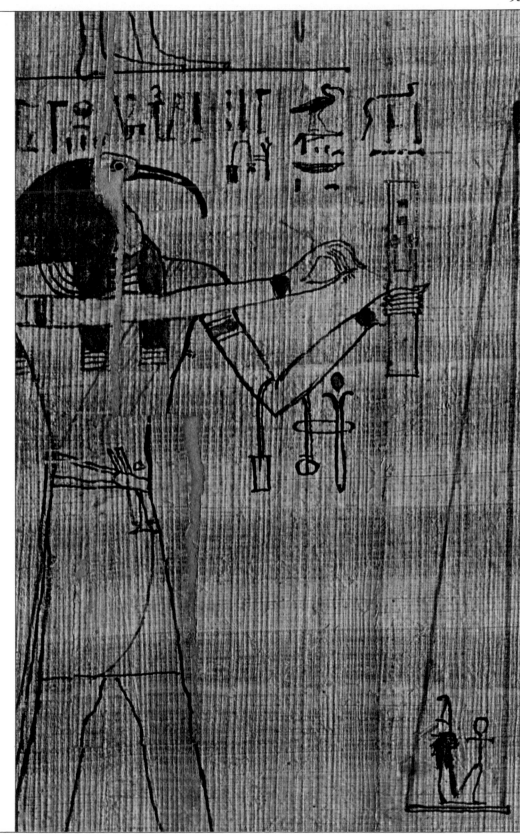

An Assortment of Palettes

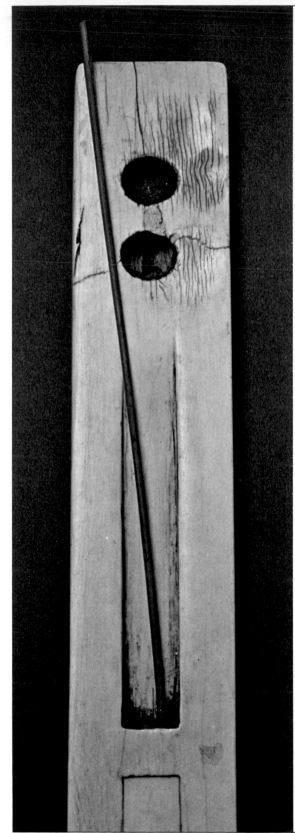

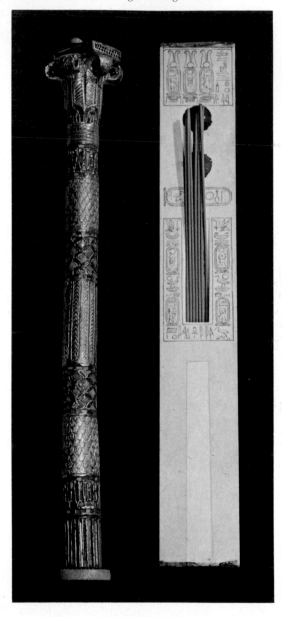

A 14-inch ivory palette (left) probably belonged to a high-ranking scribe, since most versions were made of wood. The centre slot held brushes.

King Tutankhamen's ivory palette (below) still holds its original ink cakes. The gem-inlaid case beside it carried the King's writing brushes.

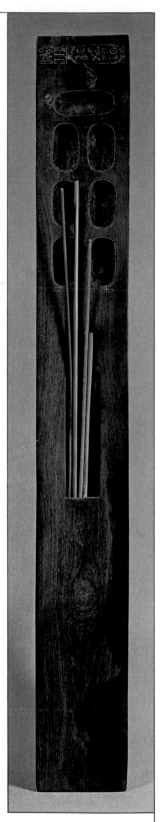

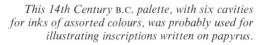

This 14th Century B.C. palette, with six cavities for inks of assorted colours, was probably used for illustrating inscriptions written on papyrus.

Mathematics was taught chiefly for its application to such practical problems as the division of fields (essential in dealing with matters of inheritance and land transfer), the computation of grain needed to sow fields of specific dimensions and the allotment of rations (equally essential for an administrator responsible for the maintenance of labourers, slaves or soldiers). Scribes had to use mathematics constantly, to add up administrative receipts and disbursements, figure interest payments on loans and calculate the quantity of bricks needed for a building of specific dimensions. For this purpose the Babylonians used a rather sophisticated system of numerical notation; they reckoned grain by a decimal system, and most other objects and concepts by a system of sixties, equivalent to the one that survives today in the measurement of time: 60 minutes in the hour, 60 seconds in the minute. They also compiled multiplication tables, and they could quite accurately determine square and cube roots.

Because they could handle such mathematical values, essential to simple plane geometry, and since they understood basic algebra, there is reason to believe that a thousand years before Pythagoras was born scribes along the Euphrates may have worked out the famous Pythagorean theorem—the square of the hypotenuse of a right-angled triangle is equal to the sum of the squares of the other two sides. And the Middle Eastern scribes eventually became quite sophisticated in astronomy, a science that depends on mathematics; evidently they were able to predict solar and lunar eclipses.

Despite this rather broad range of subjects available to students, aspiring scribes in Mesopotamia concentrated first and foremost on reading and writing. Some of the courses were of a legal nature —instructions on how to draw up and seal proper deeds, contracts and other documents. The same kinds of courses taught the jargons of various social groups—priests, judges, medicine men, smiths, merchants and shepherds. As a fully-fledged scribe, the aspirant knew he would have to deal with many sorts of men, and a knowledge of their special vocabularies and word usages would be essential.

Much of the Mesopotamian scribal student's time was also spent in learning Sumerian equivalents of Akkadian words, Sumerian grammatical terms, Sumerian verb conjugations, translation from Akkadian to Sumerian and vice versa.

Experts disagree on the date when the Sumerian tongue died out as a living language. But towards the end of the Third Millennium the southern cities, where the Sumerian people had invented cuneiform, began to go into eclipse, and at the same time a new people, settling in the northern cities of Akkad and Babylon (whence the names of the languages and the subsequent cultures), was becoming predominant. By 1800 B.C. the Sumerian tongue had been replaced by Akkadian in everyday use throughout the land.

But in the *edubba* and on royal monuments the dead Sumerian language was kept alive in one way or another for more than 1,000 years after the lapse of Sumerian from ordinary usage.

Why did Sumerian persist for so long? Religious tradition is doubtless one explanation: in copying and recopying Sumerian religious texts, the scribes may well have felt that they were serving their gods, whose deeds were first recorded in the Sumerian language. Much as Latin remained the chief liturgical

A principal rôle of scribes in ancient Egypt is memorialized
in this farm scene sculpted in wood and placed in the tomb of
a prominent nobleman named Meketre some 4,000 years ago.
Seated on a throne in his pavilion (left), Meketre watches
herdsmen drive his cattle through the yard to be counted. To
his right four scribes record the tally on papyrus sheets, while
another scribe, across the yard, assisted by two drovers,
takes an independent count as a cross-check. Such inventory
taking enabled scribes to figure the tax assessment, generally
to be paid in a percentage of the herd or other commodities.

tongue of the Western Christian Church long after worshippers had stopped speaking it, Sumerian seems to have persisted in the expression of religious ceremony in certain parts of Mesopotamia for a good many centuries past the end of its use in daily life.

But religion can hardly be the whole story, since not all the later Sumerian documents deal with religious subjects. As late as 1000 B.C. the Assyrian kings continued to use Sumerian alongside Akkadian in royal inscriptions on public buildings, though Sumerian would have been intelligible to few of the people who viewed the inscriptions. But an older language often conveys a sense of dignity suitable to monuments and public edifices. In more recent times, people everywhere have followed a similar example: many a public building from Paris to San Francisco carries a Latin inscription over its portals, as does many a university campus gate. Christian gravestones everywhere still bear the phrase *Requiescat in pace*—Latin for "rest in peace". And modern Chinese signature seals—the carved wooden, stone and jade seals used to validate legal documents—frequently indicate the signer's name in ancient pictographic signs.

In the long history of Mesopotamian schools, student scribes continued to copy out Sumerian dictionaries, grammars, commentaries on difficult words and glosses on Sumerian documents. Some of them continued to compose poetry in Sumerian until 1500 B.C. and possibly later. They also wrote countless essays —some original, some copied from Sumerian models composed by their ancestors—describing life in the scribal schools and the behaviour that was expected of the students. In a confrontation described in such

an essay on one clay tablet, a father asks his truant son: "Where did you go?" and the boy answers, "I did not go anywhere." The father then demands: "Why do you idle about? Go to school, stand before your school father, recite your assignment." He finally concludes: "Write your tablet, let your elder brother write your new tablet. After you have finished your assignment and reported to your monitor, come to me, and do not wander about in the street."

Some students, aided and abetted by their parents, went in for elaborate boot-licking. According to one clay tablet, an indulgent father invited the teacher to dinner, seated him in a comfortable chair and asked the boy to recite. The father, addressing the teacher, declared: "My little fellow has opened his hand, and you made wisdom enter there; you showed him the fine points of the scribal art; you made him see the solutions of the mathematical and arithmetical problems." This buttering-up process was not limited to mere words; the father ordered his servants to "make fragrant oil flow like water on [the teacher's] stomach and back; I want to dress him in a [new] garment, give him some extra salary, put a ring on his hand." Thus persuaded by all this flattery, the teacher praised the boy at length, declaring: "You have carried out the school's activities, you are a man of learning." It is probably safe to assume that thereafter the boy's schoolwork "improved".

In Mesopotamian schools, as in modern schools, the culmination of the student's experience was a test. Before going out into the world, the student was required to prove his learning. One clay tablet records an oral examination given by a scribe to his son—who was probably his "school son", or pupil. The examination, on all the subjects the student had learned during his school years, took place in the *edubba* courtyard before an assemblage of masters.

The young aspirant who is described on this particular clay tablet failed to pass his test. Unable to accept his flunking marks, he claimed that it was his school father and elder brothers who had failed, not he. At this, his examiner upbraided him: "What have you done, what good came of your sitting here? You are already a ripe man and close to being aged! Like an old ass, you are not teachable any more. Like withered grain you have passed the season. How long will you play around? But it is still not too late!" he asserted, holding out some hope. "If you study night and day and work all the time modestly and without arrogance, if you listen to your colleagues and teachers, you can still become a scribe."

Some students never got so far as to take the final examination; for one reason or another, many boys simply quit. Some of these dropouts may well have become public letter writers in the small towns and villages, where they subsequently came to be referred to contemptuously by their more successful contemporaries in the big cities as *dubsar hurrum*, that is, hillbilly scribes—the term *hurrum* being thought to refer to the Hurrians, a rustic people who inhabited the hill country northwest of Sumer.

Indeed, the rise of a literate class in the cities of the ancient world undoubtedly helped to emphasize social contrasts, both real and imagined, between town and country: as ever, the unlettered rustic was compared unfavourably to the sophisticated townsman; or alternatively, the simple, honest farmer was confronted by the tricky urbanite. Two thousand years after the time of Sumer, educated Athenians referred to an ignorant or stupid fellow as a Boeotian, after the near-by rural district of Boeotia, and of course the modern terms "hillbilly", "rube" and "hick" carry much the same sense of contempt.

The number of fully-fledged scribes who graduated and practised their craft was small in proportion to the population; nevertheless, the total is significant, according to a socio-economic and religious study of the Babylonian city of Sippar done by Rivkah Harris, Professor of History and Literature of Religion at Northwestern University. Dr. Harris based her study on clay tablets recording the business and legal affairs of the city between 1850 and 1550 B.C. Towards the end of that period, when it was at the height of its influence, Sippar had a population of perhaps 10,000 citizens. For the entire 300-year period she studied, Dr. Harris found the names of 185 scribes —of whom 10 were women.

The figure of 185 may seem small at first glance, but it is higher than the figures available for the practitioners of any other occupation. Dr. Harris concludes that the rate of literacy in Sippar was higher than might have been expected. But the figure may actually be too low, since it includes only those individuals whose names are explicitly designated as *dubsar*—tablet writer. Doubtless many a *dubsar* did not bother to write down his professional title, while the names of some others must have been lost along with the clay documents that bore them.

The names of other educated Babylonians, including temple administrators and schoolmasters, may never have appeared in documents at all, or at least not in any context indicating that they were literate. But even if Professor Harris' figures are multiplied by 10, the total number of literates would

How to Carve a Hieroglyph

The creation of hieroglyphs on stone called for a high degree of artistic skill. The symbols could either be incised or sculpted in bas-relief; both methods are shown on these pages. The details of owls' heads at the near right, taken from limestone slabs on which neophyte artist-scribes practised, reveal the two stages in carving a hieroglyph: roughing out the figure in ink on a rock surface, then chiselling it. At the top right corner of the illustration opposite is an exquisitely delicate example of an owl done in bas-relief. Scribes often achieved such accuracy that an exact species can be identified by zoologists.

Barn owls so closely resemble owl symbols in hieroglyphic writing that naturalists believe these animals were common in ancient Egypt. This painting, from a field guide to Egyptian birds, juxtaposes a modern owl with its hieroglyphic ancestor.

Two practice hieroglyphs—one a drawn outline of an owl's head (top) and the other a crudely carved version (bottom) —were found in temples at Thebes and Mesheikh; they record two preliminary stages in the formation of a symbol. Though the scribes were allowed certain artistic licence, convention dictated that the bird representing the sound "m" always be posed with its body in profile and its head facing forwards.

This fragment of an inscription in bas-relief, from a 4,500-year-old tomb at Gizeh, includes an owl hieroglyph of excellent craftsmanship.

still be very small when spread over a span of 300 years. Given a man's short life expectancy in those days, it is probable that no more than a few hundred literates were alive in Sippar at any given time. And in the smaller towns and countryside, of course, literates would have been even fewer.

Because learned men and women in ancient Mesopotamia were scarce, they were respected. The successful *edubba* graduate found a variety of careers open to him. He might perhaps enter the *edubba gula*, or big school, apparently a sort of university found only in the large cities—Babylon and possibly Nippur. No evidence survives to indicate what subjects these ancient colleges taught, though some likely possibilities have been advanced: astronomy, astrology and perhaps medicine.

Instead of going on with his own schooling, the graduate of a scribal academy might become a teacher, tyrannizing a generation of boys as he himself had once been tyrannized. Or he might find a job administering a large estate, or handling correspondence and contracts for a prosperous merchant or banker. He might go into business for himself, setting up as a sort of notary public who drew up and witnessed contracts, deeds and promissory notes. Well before 2000 B.C. the Sumerians had evolved written codes of law—possibly because a constant influx of peoples entering their land brought new ideas, and with them disputes over what rules and regulations should prevail. Mesopotamian courts required written evidence in cases involving disputes over land, loans and contracts.

Perhaps most important of all, the graduate of the scribal school might become a civil servant, acting as a clerk, paymaster, accountant or secretary in a temple or palace. A clever or lucky boy might rise to the position of temple administrator, ambassador or king's minister. In Mesopotamia, as in many later civilizations, much of the actual power in government was held by the professional bureaucrats rather than by the kings, generals, high priests and nobles who were nominally in charge.

In particular, the literate scribal executive assistant to a king or other top official had much to say about what written messages did or did not reach his master. A letter to Ashurbanipal, a seventh-century B.C. king of Assyria—the empire that succeeded that of Babylonia—contains a P.S. addressed to the royal secretary: "Whoever you are, scribe, who is going to read this letter, do not conceal anything from the King, my lord, so that the gods Bel and Nabu should speak kindly of you to the King."

The advice may have been merely a homily, speaking to the better nature of the royal scribe. Or it may have had sharper teeth. Certainly, for the scribe no less than for his merchant peers, the laws governing fraud were severe—though nobody knows how they were enforced, since there are no records of criminal proceedings against scribes. But Hammurabi, the Babylonian king who soon after 1800 B.C. committed to writing laws that had long been honoured orally, decreed that any judge who altered a tablet was to be deprived of his seat on the bench; and the punishment for bearing false witness (witnessing being one rôle of the scribe who wrote the tablet) was death.

Of course, the particular admonition to Ashurbanipal's scribe that he be honest may have been for the record only, since both the sender of the letter and Ashurbanipal's secretary presumably were fully

Among the many great honours accorded to the scribe Amenhotep-Son-of-Hapu was this portrait-statue found in a temple. It demonstrates the lofty status a brilliant and literate man could attain in ancient Egypt. As a young military officer, this 14th-century B.C. genius was first admired for his command of hieroglyphs; before long he was handling all manpower recruitment. Eventually the King made him collector of taxes and chief architect. The ultimate homage was a royal permit to build a funerary temple for himself. In the inscription the scribe piously offers to intercede with Amen-Re on behalf of worshippers.

aware that the King—an exception among the great men of the day—was himself able to read.

In any event, the fact that the scribe invoked the names of the gods in his letter to Ashurbanipal is an indication of the esteem in which writing was held. Bel was another name for Marduk, chief of the gods, and Nabu was the son of Marduk. Nabu was second only to his father in the pantheon. He was also scribe of the gods: as such he recorded their affairs and their decisions about the fates of men. From earliest times the scribes also had a special patroness in the goddess Nisaba; Sumerian literary texts often closed with the note "Praise be to Nisaba".

Perhaps because he fully realized the prestige of scribes, Ashurbanipal was proud of his literacy. Seventh-century B.C. inscriptions reveal that he was an accomplished scholar. He boasted that he could "read tablets written before the flood"—meaning texts that were more than 2,000 years old by his time. Ashurbanipal also spoke of himself as copying texts, an indication that writing was something that even a king felt entitled to boast about.

Whether or not Ashurbanipal was the scholar he claimed, he was incontestably the world's first large-scale book collector, and founder of the first great library. From his capital at Nineveh he sent his agents far and wide throughout Mesopotamia in search of clay tablets. One of his letters, addressed to a royal official named Shadanu, reads: "Seek out and bring me the precious tablets for which there are no transcripts existing in Assyria. I have just now written to the temple overseer and the mayor of Borsippa that you, Shadanu, are to keep the tablets in your storehouse and that nobody shall refuse to hand over tablets to you. If you hear of any tablet or ritual text that is suitable for the palace, seek it out, secure it, and send it here."

The result of such endeavours was a library of nearly 25,000 clay tablets—a large proportion of them on magical subjects (omens, astrology and incantations), but also some on medicine, astronomy and mathematics, and some embodying epic poetry, hymns and songs. Most important were the bilingual Babylonian-Sumerian dictionaries—keys to modern understanding of Sumerian. Indeed, scholars have found in this collection of clay tablets the richest mine of information unearthed anywhere on the culture of Assyria, Babylonia and Sumer. The establishment of such a library underlines an important fact about the development of writing: what had begun as a practical tool of administration and commerce had by the First Millennium B.C. come to be valued for its own sake and for the knowledge it could impart.

No such lode exists to tell of the scribes in Egypt, that other great centre of ancient writing. The hiero-glyphic inscriptions carved and painted on the walls of tombs and public buildings are concerned mainly with religious matters, and with the lives and achievements of kings and nobles. More mundane matters were recorded on sheets of papyrus, much less durable than clay tablets.

But among the papyrus fragments that do survive are essays, letters and poems glorifying the scribe and his lot in life. One essay, which may originally have been written before 2000 B.C., portrays a father taking his son to school. On the way, the parent exhorts the child on the need for diligence at his studies; the penalty of failure, the father points out, is a lifetime of back-breaking manual labour.

"I have seen the smith at his work beside his furnace," the father declares. "His fingers are like crocodile skin, and he stinks worse than fish roe." Continuing in the same disparaging vein about the stonemason, the barber and several other labourers, the father writes off the farmer, who "wears the same clothes for all seasons. His voice is raucous as a crow's. His fingers are always busy, his arms are dried up by the wind. He takes his rest—when he gets any—in the mud." The father ends by urging his son to spare no effort to become a scribe. Another papyrus concludes: "The profession of scribe is a princely profession. His writing materials and his rolls of books bring pleasantness and riches."

In Egypt, the work of the scribe might also involve travel abroad, or at least a view of the world outside. A few Egyptian scribes dealt with foreign affairs and had to learn to write Akkadian cuneiform, which served as a general diplomatic language throughout the Middle East from about 2000 to 1000 B.C. And a papyrus of 1200 B.C. tells of one scribe challenging another's knowledge of geography. Of the city of Byblos the scribe asks, "What is it like? Thou hast not trodden it." Going on to other places he says, "Pray, instruct me about Beirut, Sidon and Sarepta".

Well might he have asked. For these places, all on the Mediterranean coast just to the north and a little east of Egypt, were, in the middle of the Second Millennium B.C., outposts of Egyptian rule. They were also sought after by the Mesopotamian powers farther to the east and the Hittite Empire to the north. But these Mediterranean cities were about to free themselves of foreign rule, and to generate a cultural revolution of crucial and permanent importance to the development of writing.

Potent Magic of the Written Word

Through 3,000 years of their history in the ancient world, the Egyptians, who attributed the invention of writing to Thoth—the god of learning and wisdom—believed the written word possessed supernatural powers. Hieroglyphs, used for most religious writings and formal pronouncements (supplementing the cursive hieratic used every day), had a significance that transcended communication.

For instance, a written name embodied the essence of the person named. The name of a god carved on the columns of a temple invoked his presence. The strength of an enemy was diminished if a figurine bearing his name was smashed. And prayers and incantations, inscribed in pyramids and tombs, ensured a happy afterlife for kings and notables.

Finely carved in the shape of the hieroglyph signifying life and placed in the tomb of King Tutankhamen, this 3,450-year-old wooden case for a hand mirror is elaborately decorated with colourful inscriptions of two of the monarch's various names and titles.

The name Tutankhamen is carved in the handle. Hieroglyphs for the other name, Nebkheperure, are inlaid in glass paste at the centre of the case. The symbols supply the approximate sound of "neb" (the basket hieroglyph), "kheper" (the beetle, or scarab) and "re (the sun disc). The three strokes below the scarab signify the sound "u".

Monograms for Royalty and a Royal Servant

A gold cup bears one of King Thutmose III's official names—Menkheperre —framed in a cartouche. Inscribed above it is the phrase "the good god", referring to the King's divine status on earth; below it are hieroglyphs meaning "given enduring life", alluding to his dream of divine immortality.

A silver canister, part of a set of personal tableware from the palace of Thutmose III, came from the tomb of one of his six wives. Dated about 1460 B.C., the vessel is inscribed: "a gift from the King to the Queen Merti".

Fitted with a mirror and with jars for cosmetics in a drawer, a cedar-wood toiletry chest has inscribed on its front panel the image of its owner, a royal butler, presenting his King with a similar set of jars. Describing himself as "the true confidant of the King", the 18th-century B.C. major-domo also had his master's name—Amenemhet IV—written on the rim of the lid.

In Splendid Praise of Gods and Kings

Hieroglyphs on the near column of a Second Millennium B.C. *temple of Amen-Re extol King Senusert I (left), who offers the god gifts.*

A literate 13th-century B.C. builder of royal tombs named Peshedu designed and constructed his own. He covered the ceiling with the Litany of Re, a religious text that celebrated the Sun God's eternal passage between heaven and the underworld. He decorated the walls with pictures of gods, each one holding the sign of the hieroglyph for life.
At rear, Peshedu pictured himself surrounded by figures and symbols including that of the underworld god Osiris (centre), and the huge, all-seeing eye of the sky-god Horus, son of Osiris, which looks out for the eternal bliss of the dead.

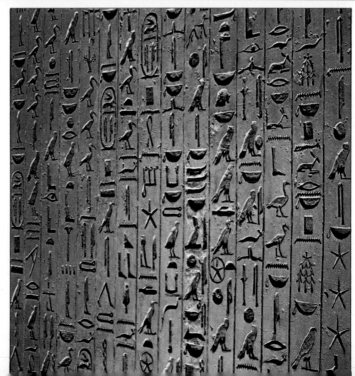

Incised on the interior walls of the 4,500-year-old pyramid of King Unas, these hieroglyphs implore the gods to receive the King as an equal. The exquisitely detailed signs were executed by artisans whose standards of workmanship over more than 2,000 years were emulated but never surpassed.

Statues of wood, stone or pottery, inscribed with the names of the deceased, were placed in the graves of wealthy Egyptians to substitute for the dead in the performance of any physical labour that might be demanded by the gods in the afterlife. These figurines, from the Second Millennium B.C., bear inscriptions identifying them as farmworkers.

By 2000 B.C. the craft of writing was more than a thousand years old. It had spread far beyond Mesopotamia and Egypt, where cuneiform and hieroglyphs had first appeared, and was in use all over the Middle East in many variations. As it spread it had changed, becoming simpler in form even as it became more complex in usage.

Over the ensuing millennium came the last and most vital step in its evolution: the advent of the alphabet. No one knows exactly when or where or by whom the first step was taken, but by the dawn of the Second Millennium several scripts were already moving in that direction, and somewhere among the forms of writing that flourished along the east coast of the Mediterranean Sea there evolved a predecessor of the Phoenician alphabet. Beginning about 1000 B.C., Phoenician traders carried their alphabet with them from the Mediterranean ports, spreading the seed for all the alphabets in use in the modern world.

What exactly is the alphabet? Seven different alphabetic scripts are employed today, but all of them rest on a single principle: an alphabet consists of a fixed set of written signs, each standing, in theory at least, for a single spoken sound; all the signs can be used interchangeably to form the various words of a given language.

In practice, few fully developed alphabets meet the ideal of one sign per sound; with the passage of time, changes in the way hands shape the signs, the effects

A text from the First Book of Samuel in late Aramaic script is preserved on three leather fragments from the Dead Sea Scrolls, found in Israel in 1952. This form of alphabetic writing, a forerunner of Hebrew and Arabic, evolved around the 10th Century B.C. It had already been widely used in the Middle East when this manuscript was written in 250 B.C.

of dialect and the voices that speak the words cause script and sounds to evolve along divergent paths. But the principle of a finite number of signs to indicate the sounds of the human voice, no matter what the language is, has remained intact.

This remarkable system arose as the result of a great burst of cultural ferment that took place over a period that lasted a thousand years or more—from about 2500 B.C.—in the region occupied today by Israel, Lebanon and Syria, bounded on the south by the Sinai Peninsula, on the north by the river Orontes and, about 50 miles inland to the east, by the mountains of Lebanon and the river Jordan.

In the Third Millennium B.C. the area was populated primarily by Semites—loosely related tribes who had originated in the Arabian Desert to the south (modern Saudi Arabia) and who had dispersed throughout the Middle East in several waves of migration beginning about 3000 B.C. The first migrants had gone east into the Sumerian cities and had taken a strong hand in the metamorphosis of Sumer into the Akkadian kingdom and into the later Babylonian and Assyrian empires. Another wave of Semitic settlers, coming soon after, travelled west to the Mediterranean, where they were to become known in Biblical times as Canaanites. Their descendants would be known to the Greeks as Phoenicians. Along the seashore they settled in a string of cities that for centuries to come were to share similar dialects, religious beliefs and mutual trading interests. Yet despite what they had in common, these cities never coalesced into an empire, though they did form an identifiable, if fragmented, civilization.

Perhaps the most significant fact about the Canaan-

Chinese: A Start with Oracles

Ranking among the most ancient of scripts, Chinese writing has preserved its essential character for more than 3,500 years. The oldest pictographs (*first column below*) have evolved into increasingly abstract and complex symbols (*second and third columns*). But partly because the Chinese resisted outside influences over long periods of time, the writing has never developed into an alphabetic system.

Since the earliest pictures could not represent abstract thoughts, or even many concrete ideas, new characters were gradually conceived to broaden the range of written communication. In the process, the number of characters used by the Chinese has grown from about 2,500 in 1400 B.C. to more than 50,000 in use today.

The flat underside of a tortoise shell, from the 14th century B.C., is incised with the oldest form of Chinese writing. Approached by a client anxious to know the future, a scribe drilled holes in the shell and carved appropriate questions on it. The shell was heated, causing cracks to fan out from the holes, and the scribe interpreted the resulting patterns.

PICTOGRAPH	CHOU ERA	MODERN
man	大	尺	人
hill	𝆄	⛰	山
tree	朱	木	木
dog	犭	犬	犬
moon	🌙	⺆	月
water	水	⚌	水
bird	🐦	鳥	鳥

The Chinese pictographs, drawn with a reed to look like the objects they represented, have culminated in highly abstract signs written with a brush.

During the middle of the Chou era (1122-256 B.C.) records of historical events and business transactions were cut into bronze vessels like this ceremonial bowl. Chou writing (centre column at left) developed from pictographs (first column).

ites was their zeal and talent for manufacture and trade. Like all ancient societies, theirs was primarily based on agriculture. But in their territories alongside the sea, agriculture was more difficult and considerably less prosperous than it was in the richer soils of Mesopotamia and Egypt. The region was too hilly for irrigation, and neither of the area's rivers —the Orontes and the Jordan—overflowed annually to fertilize the land with silt.

But if nature was unkind to the Canaanites in this respect, it profoundly blessed them in another. For the hills supported olive trees that could be cultivated for oil, cedar trees for timber and sheep for wool. Sometime during the Third Millennium—no one knows just when—the Mediterranean fishermen discovered the remarkable properties of the murex snail. A marine mollusc whose decomposing body exudes fluids coloured in hues from pink to a deep purple, the murex snail supplied vivid dyes that were highly prized by the rich. Indeed, two ancient words for purple provide the names of the peoples who lived in the region: "Canaan" derives from a Semitic word that is thought to mean "dealers in purple", and "Phoenician"—a term first used in Homer's *Iliad*—is a Greek word with the same original meaning.

The eastern Mediterranean coast was blessed with sheltered harbours that both attracted foreign traders and beckoned the inhabitants to the outside world. The coastal cities of Byblos, Ugarit, Tyre and Sidon grew up around the harbours, and together these communities formed the crossroads of the ancient world. To the east, by caravan across the mountains and by river-boat down the Euphrates, lay Mesopotamia; to the south, a short journey by way of the Sinai Peninsula and the Red Sea, was Egypt. The Hittite Empire lay along the north-eastern shore of the Mediterranean (the region of ancient Asia Minor and modern Turkey), and in the sea to the west lay Cyprus and Crete. People from all these lands had to come through the Mediterranean ports in order to trade their goods with one another.

Living in the middle of everything, the Canaanites and their Phoenician descendants were in the right place to make the most of all this trading activity: they not only exported their own products, but they also acted as agents, jobbers and shippers for the other societies on all sides. They moved copper from Cyprus (the name of the island comes from the Greek word for copper); wool, silver and tin from Asia Minor; dates, textiles and pearls from Mesopotamia; papyrus, linen, gold, ivory and incense from Egypt. The buying, selling and transporting of these commodities—by ship, donkey and muleback—vastly enriched the rulers of these coastal cities.

Yet the geographical importance and the wealth of the eastern Mediterranean communities were mixed blessings. The coast was of strategic as well as commercial interest to the lands on all sides, which sought control of the coastal ports and the mountain passes not only in order to secure their own trade routes but also to deny both ports and passes to their rivals. Egypt, in periods of power and prosperity, pushed up the coast; Mesopotamian rulers and Hittite kings of Asia Minor pressed in from the east and north. The area was a natural invasion route for all these peoples when they went to war with one another—as they frequently did; and all of them periodically held one or more of the cities under their imperial thumbs. In addition, desert nomads made occasional raids, and so did peoples from the sea.

Thus life in the Canaanite cities was dangerous and uncertain. But the constant flow into the region of different peoples created polyglot communities where men and women of half a dozen disparate origins jostled one another in narrow streets filled with the shouts of vendors and the odours of spices, cooking oil and garlic. In their comings and goings, they added their dialects, customs and cultural inventions to the life of the Canaanite ports, making them a seedbed of cultural growth as well as material wealth.

Nowhere is this ferment more evident than in the art of writing. In a mere thousand years or less, this one region—a strip stretching only 500 miles along the coast and reaching just a few miles inland—produced several distinctive scripts. Whether, and to what extent, the scripts borrowed directly from Egyptian and Mesopotamian writing is to scholars a vexing question. What is certain is that among these modes of writing are to be found the roots of all modern alphabet systems, which evolved from the Phoenician.

Three ancient scripts in particular incorporate combinations of tantalizing traits—the form and number of the characters, the sounds they express, the sequences they follow, even the names of the characters themselves—that mark them as possible predecessors of the Phoenician alphabet that finally emerged about 1100 B.C.

Of the three, perhaps the oldest is the so-called Byblos pseudohieroglyphic script, whose origin, language, uses—even the time in which it flourished and its eventual fate—are all in dispute. It has been found incised on several tablets in Byblos, a city that was, on and off, essentially an Egyptian colony during the period from 2600 to 1800 B.C. The tablets are not clay; some are stone, six are bronze—and both media are uncommon in this area. That is one reason why they are difficult to date; stone and bronze are not susceptible to dating by laboratory analysis as are clay and wood. Another reason is that the inscriptions are too few and too brief to be read; there is no clue to their dates in the wording. Finally, the tablets have been found in scattered places, with no other artifacts alongside to reveal what might have been contemporaneous with them.

The enigmatic script of Byblos is called pseudohieroglyphic because some of the signs vaguely resemble Egyptian hieroglyphs. Altogether the characters employed total only about 80: by comparison the hieroglyphs and cuneiform signs then in use still numbered several hundred. The script must have been syllabic, since 80 characters are too few for a pictographic script but too many for an alphabet. The crucial fact about the Byblos script is that scribes had learned to make fewer characters do more work.

When did the people of Byblos learn to do so? Some scholars put the date as early as 2100 B.C., when cuneiform in Mesopotamia was becoming syllabic; some experts make it as late as 1300 B.C., when writing elsewhere was already becoming alphabetic.

Either way, the Byblos inscriptions raise interesting questions about where that script falls in the overall evolutionary course of writing—and of the alphabet in particular. Did the scribes of Byblos in taking over some symbols from hieroglyphs also take over the phonetic values of the same hieroglyphs? In other words, where the Egyptians used a picture of a viper to represent the sound "f", did the scribes of Byblos do likewise? Or did they simply adopt Egyptian pictures of animals, but then apply to them the names

The simplicity of an alphabet brought writing closer to ordinary men and permitted them to indulge the immemorial urge to write graffiti. This inscription around a crude sketch of a camel (centre) and engraved on a stone by a Bedouin in the Second Century A.D. *is in Safaitic, an early Arabic script. Its message conveys the writer's pride of authorship: "Malik, son of Hasibat, son of Abd, made this picture of the young she-camel."*

of the same creatures in their own language? Both phenomena have occurred in the history of writing.

Byblos is also the city in which the earliest evidence of the Phoenician alphabet has been found and, therefore, presumably the port from which the alphabet was exported to the rest of the world. Is there a traceable connection between the pseudohieroglyphs and the Phoenician alphabet? No one knows, though the likeness of three Byblos signs to Phoenician letters indicates the possibility.

Some scholars have placed the beginnings of the alphabet at another outpost of Egyptian rule: the Sinai Peninsula, where for some 400 years, between 1800 and 1400 B.C., Semites in the employ of Egyptians mined copper and turquoise. On the quarried walls, the miners left behind some 50 mysterious inscriptions, together with statues of a goddess. Though the signs are pictorial, bearing some resemblance to Egyptian hieroglyphs, the script consists of only 27 different signs—an enormous reduction from the hundreds of hieroglyphs. It is hard to escape the conclusion that the signs—which have not yet been deciphered—represent an alphabetic or nearly alphabetic script. And if, as most scholars believe, the inscriptions belong to the 15th Century B.C., they are among the earliest alphabetic signs yet found.

Translations of no more than a few of the characters have been made. But from those that have been figured out comes one of the most interesting —though not universally accepted—theories about the origin of the alphabet: that the Sinaitic Semites, under Egyptian influence, devised an alphabet by arbitrarily assigning to Egyptian hieroglyphs spoken Semitic words for 27 of the commonest objects in their own daily life. To name the four most appropriate examples: the ox, the house, the camel and the door. Thus this theory, which achieved its greatest currency about the turn of this century, argues that the Semites gave each of the signs for ox, house, camel and door their Semitic names: alef, bet, gamel, dalet. Clearly, then those names would be the forerunners of the Phoenician aleph, beth, gamel, daleth, which would later become the Greek alpha, beta, gamma and delta, whence came A, B, C and D.

The fact that the script was in use geographically, midway between Egypt and the Phoenician ports, lends further weight to the theory that the baffling Sinaitic inscriptions may represent the missing link between hieroglyphs and the Phoenician alphabet. The marked resemblance of some of the signs to Egyptian hieroglyphs adds to the evidence.

All in all, a neat explanation—but it suffered disarray with the discovery, at the land of Canaan's northern end, of another script that was different from the Sinaitic, though just as old.

In the north-west corner of Syria, the town of Ras Shamra stands upon the site of the ancient port of Ugarit—a fact not suspected until one day in 1928 when a farmer tending his fields stumbled upon a subterranean chamber. Ensuing excavations by French scholars turned up a temple so magnificent it was at first mistaken for a palace. In princely graves were found vases, jewels and statuary imported from Egypt, Mesopotamia, Asia Minor, Cyprus and Crete and, most important, thousands of clay tablets. About a hundred of those tablets were still lying in the kiln where they had been placed for firing. Among them was a letter from the King of Ugarit to a neighbouring

ruler refusing a request for food and ships, saying he had none to spare because his own city was being threatened by an enemy he did not name, but known to the Egyptians as Peoples of the Sea and to the Israelites as Philistines.

Most of the tablets found in Ugarit dated from the 14th Century B.C., though some went back to the 15th Century. Many were inscribed in cuneiform, as might be expected in a city of that era that traded widely and actively. But some of the tablets, including a copy of the hard-pressed King's letter, bore a puzzling unfamiliar script. Its characters, though composed of lines pressed into the clay by a wedge-shaped stylus, as are cuneiform signs, were unlike any cuneiform symbols known to modern decipherers. The characters numbered only 30, almost as few as those of the Sinaitic script.

But here, for a surprising change, was a previously undiscovered writing system that could be deciphered—and was, a great deal faster than any other ancient script ever had been.

One reason for the rapid decipherment was the genius of the man who undertook the task, an erudite German recluse by the name of Hans Bauer. Gifted, as a fellow German scholar put it, with an instinct "for the mysterious cogs and internal movement of a language", Bauer was also knowledgeable in astronomy, zoology, medieval philosophy and languages that ranged from Chinese, Korean and Malay to several Semitic dialects. Armed with all this learning, he first applied himself to tedious weeks of labour —counting the frequencies of all the characters and then numbering the combinations of signs that occurred as prefixes and suffixes. Suspecting at that stage of his work that the language was a Canaanite

Text continued on page 124

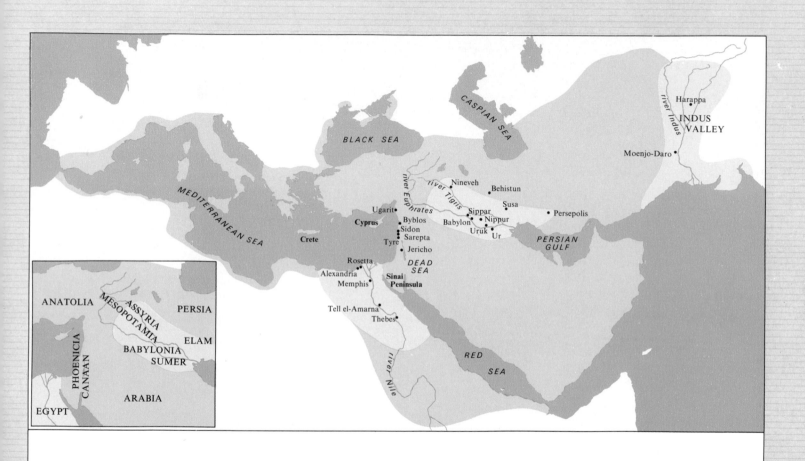

HOW THE ALPHABET EXPANDED LITERACY

The cultural impact of alphabetic writing, based on its greater simplicity and facility of learning, is charted on the map above. Until the introduction of an alphabet in the Second Millennium B.C., literacy had been generally restricted to small population pockets (*orange*) concentrated around the Nile, Indus, and Tigris and Euphrates rivers. By 400 B.C., when the Phoenician alphabet and several others had developed fully, writing had spread in an area (*green*) that covered not only the Middle East but also all the land rimming the Mediterranean. Lands and cultures that nurtured the birth and growth of writing are located in the inset map.

☐ Extent of literacy around 1600 B.C.

☐ Extent of literacy around 400 B.C.

A Variety of Famous Firsts

The inscribed objects on these pages—found in the Middle East, Greece and Rome—represent milestones in the long evolution of the written word. The inscriptions on the three artifacts below mark advances in the use of the alphabet; the two opposite, progress in expressing connected ideas and in using punctuation. The earliest find dates from about 2500 B.C.; the latest from 700 B.C.

This four-and-a-half-inch gold pin, from the seventh century B.C., *is the oldest record of the Latin alphabet. Found in Latium in 1877, it reads "Marius made me for Numerius".*

An eighth-century B.C. *vase from Athens, inscribed with the earliest Greek letters yet discovered, was probably a prize in a contest—dedicated to "him who dances most delicately".*

A calendar for farmers, this 3,000-year-old limestone tablet bears the most ancient Early Hebrew text yet found.

This Third Millennium B.C. *cuneiform inscription, on the "stone of vultures", records the victory of Lagash over Umma. The text (upper right) is the oldest employing sequential sentences.*

On the Moabite stone, dating from 850 B.C., *scholars can detect the first punctuation—vertical lines between phrases. The Semitic script recounts King Moab's war on the Israelites.*

dialect, he thereupon translated the script in only a few days' time. Though the shapes were unique, most of the signs stood for sounds corresponding to those represented by modern Hebrew and Arabic—similarities that helped Bauer enormously.

Beyond its rapid decipherment, another surprise lay in the substance of the Ugaritic inscriptions. For, together with the expected commercial correspondence, tax accounts and other governmental business records were many religious texts. And among the latter were some that bore striking similarities—not only in theme, but even in phrasing—to stories that Westerners know from the chapters of Exodus, Judges, Deuteronomy, Isaiah, Proverbs, the Song of Songs and the Book of Job; these, of course, came to the West via the Old Testament, which was first recorded in Hebrew. Scholars were thus confronted with new and exciting evidence that Biblical themes had been put down in writing many centuries earlier than had previously been thought.

But that was not the only surprise. Eventually excavators ran across the oldest-known ABC: a list of signs written in a standard order. Neither hieroglyphs nor cuneiform signs had ever been so organized (students learned them by classification—that is, in groups of animals, groups of plants and groups of other similar objects). The ABC was a stunning find —even though it came too late to help Bauer with his translations. (In the absence of such a list, even when scholars resort to the painstaking counting process employed by Bauer, they can only estimate the total number of signs, because a few occur only rarely—as do the letters Z and J in the Latin alphabet.)

The Ugaritic ABC was also important because it demonstrated that the letters of the Ugaritic script

Two Middle Eastern countries, each proud of its historic contribution to the development of the alphabet, issued these commemorative stamps. At the top is a 1956 Syrian issue showing the Second Millennium B.C. Ugaritic alphabet, written in cuneiform script on a clay tablet. Beneath it is a 1966 Lebanese stamp illustrating the ancient Phoenician alphabet—ancestor of the Greek and Latin alphabets in use today.

had fallen into a set sequence no later than the 14th Century B.C.—an impressive indication of orderliness and standardization for so early a date. Most helpful to decipherers, the tablet had the Ugaritic letters arranged opposite a column of known Babylonian syllabic signs, which supplied the sounds for the characters a, be, ga—and so on—in basically the same order and roughly the same sounds that would appear 300 years later in the Phoenician alphabet.

But for all the knowledge thus gained, the Ugaritic script, like so many others of the ancient past, remains an enigma. It recorded the phonetics of a Canaanite dialect that was much the same as the spoken Phoenician language, but its signs resemble neither those of the Phoenician alphabet nor those of any other Semitic scripts then used along the Mediterranean. And although Ugaritic was written on clay tablets with a reed stylus, the symbols look no more like cuneiform signs than Latin letters brushed on silk would look like Chinese characters. Written Ugaritic seems to stand alone. It is a fully developed system of writing that has no visible antecedents and no contemporary relatives.

The fate of the script is as mysterious as its origin. The enemy whom the Ugaritic king and his neighbours had seen coming did indeed sack and burn the city of Ugarit, destroying it with a sudden blow soon after 1200 B.C. The script disappeared with the city and left no known descendants.

But the archaeological record reveals that by 1000 B.C. the Phoenician alphabet had come to full flower; and if its origins remain mysterious, its fate is well known. It appeared first in the city of Byblos—the same city in which pseudohieroglyphs had surfaced some centuries before. Byblos is also the city that gave the Greeks a word for "papyrus scroll", by which they meant a book, and from that name also comes the English word "Bible".

In Byblos, on a stone sarcophagus that was ornately carved about 1000 B.C. with human figures portraying a funeral procession, appears a portentous inscription. It says: "The coffin which Ittobal, son of Ahiram, King of Byblos, made for his father as his abode in eternity. And if any king or any governor or any army commander attacks Byblos and exposes this coffin, let his judicial sceptre be broken, let his royal throne be overthrown and let peace flee from Byblos; and as for him, let a vagabond efface his inscriptions!" Ahiram's tomb was disturbed by robbers again and again throughout history long before archaeologists found it in the 1920s. But the royal remains have had a long life in another respect. For the inscription put there by Ahiram's son is expressed in the oldest-known linear—that is, non-pictographic —alphabet with a direct line of living descendants.

Ahiram's time was the heyday of Phoenician trade; Phoenician merchants, free of foreign rule and protected by their own local kings and by strong city trading syndicates, travelled an arc of about 2,500 miles, which stretched the entire length of the Mediterranean to its most western reach in Spain.

Where the Phoenicians travelled they carried their alphabet with them. As they did, new scribes who took it up added their own refinements—here embellishing, there paring—and everywhere making from that single script a sturdy communication tool that would survive and lend itself to any language spoken by man. In the East it evolved into Aramaic, which further developed into the Indian, Persian, Arabic and Hebrew alphabets. In the West it evolved into the Greek alphabet, which inspired first the Etruscan and then the Latin alphabet, which is used for the languages of western Europe; and later the Cyrillic alphabet, used in Slavic nations.

This fertile Phoenician alphabet that begat so many offspring was a script of 22 characters, and it was a modern alphabet in all respects but one: it had consonants but no vowels. The multitude of anonymous scribes whose combined efforts now covered 2,000 years had brought writing to a point of expressing most of the sounds they could hear in their own speech. But the human voice makes two different kinds of sounds: vowels, which are formed simply by the motion of the vocal chords alone, and consonants, which are formed by the vocal chords in combination with the tongue, the teeth or the lips, movements that either initiate the sound (as in speaking the word "tea") or terminate it (as in speaking the word "eat").

It remained for the Greeks, whose language was an Indo-European tongue, to make that distinction by supplying their own alphabet with five vowels—a feat they had accomplished by the ninth century B.C.

The Greeks themselves gave credit to the Phoenicians, however, for the invention that they built upon: they called their script Phoenician writing, and the names they assigned the letters—alpha, beta, gamma, delta—clearly derived from those the Phoenicians had inherited from their Semitic kinsmen.

How the Phoenicians and their Semitic relatives got along without vowels in their written languages (the original aleph was not a vowel like the letter A, but a sort of breathy pause between consonants) is a source of scholarly dispute. The simplest explanation is that the reader could supply the vowels from the context, just as the modern reader mentally supplies missing letters in abbreviations.

Once it was launched, the alphabet spread rapidly. By the fifth century B.C., though many Middle Eastern contracts and receipts were still executed in cuneiform, the same documents carried a notation of their substance in the Aramaic alphabet, inked on to the tablet with a brush. At the beginning of the Christian era, Aramaic largely displaced cuneiform, even in Mesopotamia, where cuneiform had originated and where it hung on longest. In a few more centuries the Coptic alphabet—sprung from the Greek—would displace hieroglyphs in Egypt.

The institution of the alphabet, with its economy of symbols, its flexibility and its direct relationship to the sounds of spoken language, made writing far easier to learn and manage. As one result, literacy spread dramatically (*page 121*); as another consequence, literate people could extend the uses of writing far beyond its utilitarian rôle as a means of transacting business and storing information. All sorts of oral traditions—fables, myths and bodies of religious belief—were waiting to be written down; with the coming of the alphabet many such inheritances saw their first organized expression in writing. Among them were the tales of war and exile in Homer's *Iliad* and *Odyssey*—resources indispensable to man's study of his own mysterious past—and the seminal books of the Old Testament.

But the coming of the alphabet was far from signifying the first emergence of such historic literary works. Those beginnings go a great deal further back, almost to the birth of writing itself.

Intricate Challenge of Decipherment

The cryptanalyst who is huddled over a cipher and the scholar-linguist who is studying an ancient writing system in a quiet library face essentially the same task. To break either cipher or inscription, the time-consuming process of counting character frequencies is indispensable. Because this is so, chances for success improve in proportion to the length and numbers of the mysterious inscriptions.

Neither the cryptanalyst nor the scholar need be fluent in the language he is trying to decipher, but he must then accumulate as much historical detail as possible. If, therefore, he encounters a specimen like the Phaistos disc (*right*), which represents the only example of its script ever found, he faces almost certain defeat. Furthermore, even if he has access to thousands of specimens, he may only manage to solve parts of the language puzzle. With one splendid exception, the writings on the pages that follow have produced that frustration.

Found at the site of the Minoan palace (right) in Phaistos, Crete, this round clay tablet from 1600 B.C. is inscribed on both sides with a text that spirals from rim to centre. Although the disc's 45 pictorial signs bear some vague resemblances to the characters in other Cretan scripts, they have stubbornly resisted all attempts at decipherment.

The Indus Script: A Resort to Computers

In the early '60s, independent teams of Finnish and Russian scholars decided to apply modern technology to decipherment of a 4,500-year-old script from the Indus Valley in Pakistan and India, written on seals like the three shown on these pages.

Some 300 signs culled from 2,000 Indus inscriptions were given numerical equivalents and programmed into computers. The machines then calculated the number of times a single figure turned up—for example, the comb on the seal (*below, right*).

These tabulations suggested that some signs represented two different words with similar sounds (such as "cede" and "seed"). Both teams then turned their attention to the modern Dravidian languages of India. There they found many word pairs with the same sound, like *pentika* (comb) and *penti* (woman), and concluded the lost language was proto-Dravidian.

The Finns continue the slow work of aligning paired words in Dravidian with signs in the Indus inscriptions, but most scholars elsewhere in the world doubt that the script will ever finally submit to this process.

The site of one of the world's oldest cities, Moenjo-Daro in Pakistan's river Indus Valley, has yielded hundreds of small carved stone pieces, thought to be signature seals, that incorporate brief inscriptions on their top edges. The culture that made them thrived between 2500 B.C. and 1800 B.C.

Comb-woman

Carved from soapstone, the Indus seals are about one inch
square and often feature the images of animals, as do the
three on these pages: a unicorn (above), rhinoceros (left, top)
and elephant. The script above them was read from right
to left and was, therefore, carved in reverse order as shown.

Mayan Hieroglyphs: Signs in Infinite Combinations

The Mayan languages, having evolved over 26 centuries, are still spoken in southern Mexico and Central America. But their written form has undergone a startling change: the ancient hieroglyphs have been totally abandoned in favour of the Latin alphabet.

Although the body of knowledge dealing with Mayan languages during the last four centuries has provided valuable clues to the concepts recorded by the hieroglyphs, many of the signs remain untranslated. The principal difficulty is their sheer number. There are about 350 main symbols that can be combined with equally numerous subsidiary symbols to form extremely complex additional signs.

Decipherers have also been hampered by a scarcity of written documents; the Spaniards destroyed nearly all these when they arrived in Mexico in the 16th Century. Surviving are only three almanacs that forecast the omens each day for crops, fishing or weather, and recorded the movements of the sun, the moon and the planet Venus (*specimens at right*). The illustrations shown are based on religious themes.

The observatory at Chichén Itzá, Yucatán, built in A.D. 900, has numerous windows whose sophisticated alignments enabled the Mayans to study the positions of celestial bodies and to produce an accurate calendar.

One of the few remaining examples of Mayan hieroglyphic documents is the Dresden Codex, a sacred almanac named for the city where it now reposes. The two pages at right predicted that disaster would follow the rising of the planet Venus on two different days. A dot represents the number one; a bar, the number five; and the shell-like shape, zero.

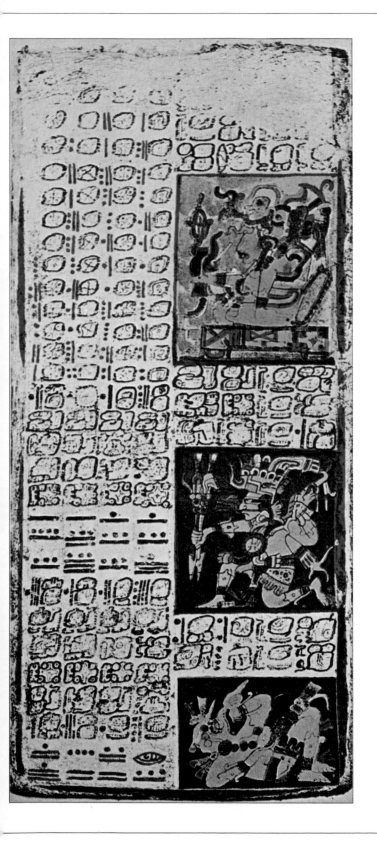

Etruscan: An Alphabet for an Unknown Language

Reading the inscriptions of the Etruscan people, who dominated northern Italy before Roman times, would seem to be easy: the script is written in Greek characters. But the language is puzzling; no clear relationship between Etruscan and any other language has ever been established.

More than 10,000 inscriptions have been found, but most are funerary epitaphs—each bearing only the dead person's name and title, his age and parentage. Nevertheless, since the late 19th Century scholars have managed to build up a vocabulary of about 200 words. Hopes of lengthening the list and supplying a structure of grammar and syntax soared in 1964 after a 36-word text came to light at the ancient port of Pyrgi. It appeared on a gold tablet, found very near another tablet similar in size, written in Phoenician, a readable language.

Scholars sniffed the possibility of the linguists' grail: a bilingual text. But they were wrong. Although both tablets recorded the dedication of the same sanctuary, the texts were not identical, and the Etruscan language remains a puzzle.

In the sixth-century B.C., *Pyrgi, located 25 miles west of Rome, was a major Etruscan seaport and religious centre. The site lies close to the present town of Santa Severa, whose castle stands on a promontory above the sea.*

Dating from 500 B.C., *these two golden tablets inscribed in Phoenician (near right) and Etruscan were dedicated to a goddess by an Etruscan king, marking his third year on the throne. Though the tablets record the same message and the Phoenician can be read, study has added only one word to the known Etruscan vocabulary: the number three.*

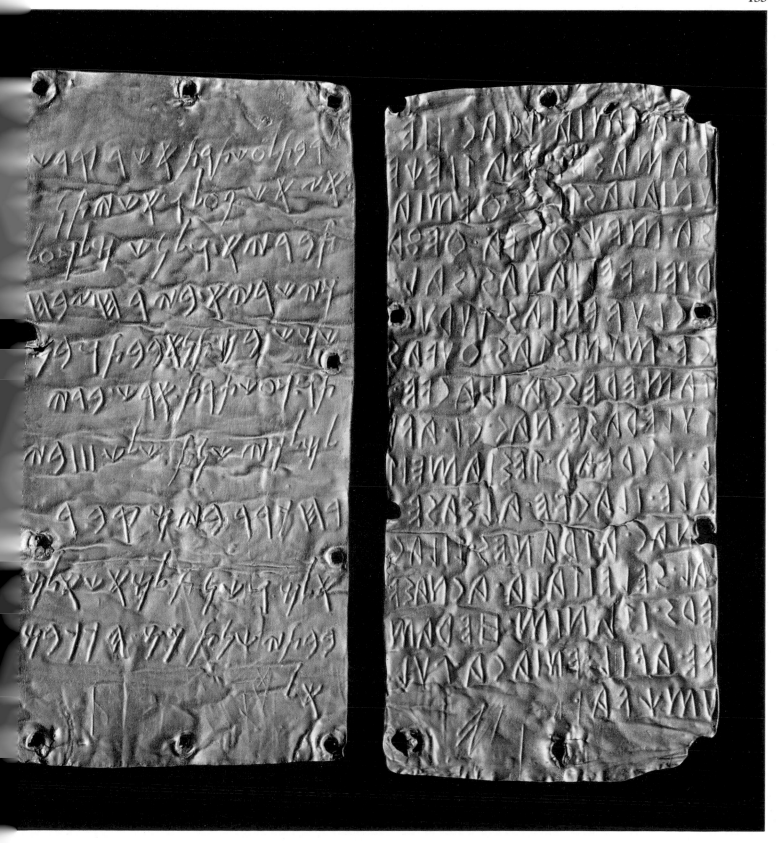

Linear B: A Triumphant Breakthrough

To scholars, the rare success of unlocking a mute script ranks with the conquest of Mount Everest. Such was the decipherment of Linear B, the cursive Minoan script that was found on Crete in 1900 and broken in 1952 by Michael Ventris—a linguistically gifted British architect.

Luckily for Ventris, hundreds of clay tablets, miraculously preserved by the fire that destroyed the Cretan palace at Knossos about 1400 B.C., bore inscriptions in Linear B, including the records of business transactions and palace inventories.

Having determined that there were 88 signs in Linear B, Ventris devised a syllabic grid with vowels across the top and consonants down the side, creating a checkerboard of suggested phonetic values for 68 signs. Then the breakthrough came: he realized that Linear B was an archaic form of Greek. To be sure, it was a dialect 1,000 years older than that used by Plato, but the grid worked. A year later the American archaeologist Carl Blegen tackled the Linear B tablet shown below and, using Ventris' system, translated it independently.

From store rooms in the palace at Knossos, Crete (shown partly reconstructed, above), came 1,800 clay tablets written in Linear B.

Carl Blegen used this tablet—a lengthy inventory of pots, written in Linear B and discovered at Pylos—to confirm Ventris' theory.

In 1953, a year after presenting his evidence that Linear B was a form of archaic Greek, Michael Ventris prepares materials —including his syllabic grid and numerous inscriptions collected in the book, foreground—for a lecture series on his discovery. He was to die in a motoring accident three years later. The so-called Linear A script, unearthed in other tablets also found in 1900 on Crete, remains untranslated.

The jumbled wedges on a battered cuneiform tablet and the painted pictures on an Egyptian tomb wall, or on a crumbling papyrus scroll, provide incomparable windows on the past; they allow the living to see and hear the images and voices of long-departed peoples who, in their time, confronted the immemorial problems of coping with nature, of getting and spending, of friendship and love, of evil and death. Their writings—ranging from funerary texts to myths and fables—become a kind of time machine, exerting new influences on contemporary man, shaping the ways in which he thinks and feels about his own crowded place in the chain of life.

At first glance, the first literate men and women seem, in some respects, very strange. They were, of course, ignorant of innumerable facts that are taken for granted today; their lives, so interlaced with superstitions, were circumscribed by custom, ritual and tradition to a degree that the modern citizen finds difficult to comprehend.

Furthermore, even scholars—fortified though they may be by years of study and by sharing one another's work—find that grasping the mere gist of many ancient writings is an enormously difficult task. For all their experience and knowledge, the translators' unfamiliarity with ancient idiom and usage, and with the thought patterns of the time, presents a tangle of problems that must be doggedly solved

This bronze statuette of a worshipper, cast about 1750 B.C., bears an inscription wishing long life to Hammurabi, King of Babylonia, who left one of the earliest written codes of law and also an extensive legacy of personal letters on religion and government. The figure, made for a temple at Larsa, may represent either the donor of the statuette or Hammurabi himself. Its hands and face are covered in gold leaf.

—one by one. And even when those difficulties are satisfactorily met, the scholars' dedication to precision in their work often results in fearsomely stilted translations that can only approximate the originals.

Given these considerations, the wonder is that the first literate voices are audible at all. But audible they are—sometimes only faintly; but just as often, loud and clear. When scribes finally passed beyond utilitarian record keeping and addressed themselves to literature, they recorded the passions of their times —the fears, hopes, joys and angers—in an astonishing variety of forms.

Because kings were paramount, documents exalting them and their deeds abound. But the oldest literature of Egypt and Mesopotamia also includes many prayers and ritual incantations, as well as chronicles, proverbs, personal letters, love lyrics, and epic poems and heroic fables. The range of subject matter can only be suggested in a necessarily limited sampling. But the excitement of becoming acquainted with human beings who lived so many centuries ago, of savouring their attitudes and moods, is quickly reinforced by reading even the few translations that can be presented here.

There is, as a first example, Hammurabi, a Babylonian king of the 18th century B.C. Celebrated by ancient scribes as among the greatest of kings, Hammurabi is credited with decreeing the first comprehensive written code of law. In its preamble, the modern reader quickly comes to appreciate not only the awesome majesty of the monarch's personality but also the striking modernity of his ideas and their phrasing. Hammurabi describes himself as "the ancient seed of royalty, the powerful king, the son of

Babylon"—thus establishing his credentials as a law-giver. It was the gods, he goes on to say, who "named me to promote the welfare of the people, to cause justice to prevail in the land, to destroy the wicked and the evil, that the strong might not oppress the weak".

A pharaoh like Thutmose III, who considered himself a god as well as a king, had no need to attribute his worth to higher beings. Of the 15th century B.C. monarch's prowess as a hunter, for example, an inscription by an adulatory scribe claims that Thutmose could with aplomb bag more animals than his entire army; and on one occasion "he killed seven lions in a moment and carried off a herd of 12 wild cattle in an hour after breakfast".

Documents invoking the good will of the gods frequently are entreaties for clemency and peace that transcend time, and their cadence is comfortable to any religious person today:

My merciful lady—my lady be calm!
My lady who does not become angry, who is calm.
My lady who gives, my lady who is so very good.

On a more earthly level, bulky compilations of proverbs were a special delight of the Egyptians. As set forth in the words of a Third Millennium B.C. royal official named Ptah-hotep, the advice was indeed pithy and sound: "If you are one of those sitting at table with one greater than yourself, take what he may give when it is set before your nose. Laugh after he laughs, and it will be very pleasing to his heart." Ptah-hotep also advises those who want to make a good relationship last: "In a home to which you have access as a son, a brother or as a friend, beware of approaching the women."

Finally, there is the ultimate confirmation that, through the ages, letters from children to their parents have not changed that much. The son of a high official under Hammurabi wrote to his mother: "May my father and the gods keep you well. Gentlemen's clothes improve year by year. But you are making my clothes cheaper year by year. The son of Adad-iddinam, whose father is a mere underling of my father, has received two new garments, but you keep getting upset over just one garment for me. Though you gave birth to me, his mother adopted him; whereas his mother loves him, you do not love me."

The love lyrics of the ancient world consistently reflect a deep appreciation of nature; with their references to horses and deer and birds—used as metaphors for the beloved or the feeling of love—they prefigure the Biblical Song of Songs. Nevertheless, as literature they seem pallid beside two other poetic forms. Such poems are direct descendants of the oral traditions of myth and fable that were the sources of ancient religion and philosophy, and which antedate writing in all ancient civilizations. Long before writing emerged, priests in the temples of Egypt and Mesopotamia inspired the faithful with sonorous prayers addressed to the gods. In the market-places, story-tellers entertained passers-by and loiterers with tales of gods and demons and of how the world began. These fanciful thoughts were set in rhythmic and colourful language that lifted the spirits of the listeners and rendered the prayers and the tales, which were often long, easy to remember.

Before the end of the Second Millennium, as writing became an effective vehicle for communicating thoughts and feelings, the oldest oral traditions were set down for posterity. Among them were archetypes

Tablet fragment, actual size

More than 30 lines of a poetic cycle about Inanna, the Sumerian goddess of love, were translated in 1959 from a tablet covered with the tiniest cuneiform writing ever found. The part of her story that appears here is a fragment of a much larger clay tablet dating from about 1800 B.C., excavated at Lagash, Iraq. The fragment, enlarged three times below, is only a minuscule fraction of the several thousand lines of narrative poetry that the original document bore when intact. The almost microscopic symbols that crowd the clay surface were probably written by a scribe looking through a pair of hollow reeds, held in one hand, to help focus his eyes while he impressed the wedges with his other hand.

that would become the staples of literature everywhere, with themes upon which the heirs of the Egyptian and Mesopotamian civilizations were to build for thousands of years to come. They included the epic, based on a human figure of heroic proportions, and the myth, which tried to explain the mysteries of fertility and death. Both forms resounded with the echoes of the oral literature from which they were born, and indeed many of the tales continued to be recited aloud long after they had been inscribed on clay and papyrus. But before the end of the First Millennium B.C., many of them had found some expression in writing.

The oldest-known tale centring on a hero who is essentially human—though since he is partly divine, he dallies with gods and mythical monsters—is the *Epic of Gilgamesh.* Probably originally written about 2000 B.C., it survives in several ancient versions. The most complete and best preserved rendition appears on 12 clay tablets composed by Babylonian scribes; the manuscript was found in the library established by the Assyrian king Ashurbanipal at Nineveh in the seventh century B.C. But the elements of the story trace back to Sumerian times—a fact that can be discerned from the names of the characters and the places they frequent. Gilgamesh, the hero, is thought to have grown from the folk memory of a real king who ruled the Sumerian city of Uruk about 2600 B.C.

The tale recounts the wanderings of Gilgamesh, who leaves his home in Uruk searching for the secret of immortality, but in the end finds serenity in resigning himself to the knowledge that immortality is out of man's reach. On the way to attaining that serenity, however, he passes through many adventurous episodes of human love, friendship, fierce combat and the constant search for knowledge.

Like all such heroes of literature everywhere —from Odysseus to Tarzan—Gilgamesh is physically powerful and sexually irresistible. He is "fearsome like a wild ox" and he "leaves not the maid to her mother, nor the warrior's daughter, nor the noble's spouse". Because his invincibility poses a threat to gods as well as men, the Sumerian mother-goddess, Aruru, creates a rival to hold him in check. She does so casually, by pinching a bit of clay and throwing it out upon the wild plains. There the clay grows into a peaceable if awesome creature—a wild and totally uncivilized man.

A passage adapted from a translation of the poem by the Babylonian scholar E. A. Speiser describes the creature, whose name is Enkidu:

Shaggy with hair is his whole body,
He is endowed with head hair like a woman.
He knows neither people nor land.
With the gazelles he feeds on grass,
With the wild beasts he jostles at the
    watering place.

Though Enkidu avoids people, a hunter complains to Gilgamesh that the monster is protecting the wild animals, thereby making it impossible to hunt:

"I am so frightened that I dare not
    approach him.
He filled in the pits that I had dug,
He tore up my traps which I had set,
The beasts and creatures of the plain
He has made to slip through my hands."

Clearly, the hunter expects Gilgamesh to go forth and slay this wild man; instead, the King exhorts the hunter to participate in a wily plan:

"Go, take with you a pleasure girl.
When Enkidu appears with the beasts at the
    watering place,
She shall pull off her clothing, and
As soon as he sees her he will draw near to her."

The hunter duly engages a pleasure girl (a temple prostitute) and returns with her to the watering place. There they wait two days until Enkidu appears. The hunter urges the woman to seduce Enkidu—and she easily does so. "The barbarous fellow from the depths of the plain" is charmed by the first woman he has ever seen. For six days and seven nights they make love. Finally, he looks for his friends the wild beasts only to find that, as Gilgamesh had anticipated, his week of human companionship has made the animals suspicious of him. But the woman reassures him that he has not lost anything:

"You are wise, Enkidu, you are become like a god!
Why roam with the wild creatures?
Come, let me lead you to the city of Uruk,
To the holy temple, abode of the gods,
Where lives Gilgamesh, accomplished in strength,
And like a wild ox lords it over the people."
Her words found favour, his heart was enlightened,
He yearned for a friend.

Having agreed to go with the woman, Enkidu expects he will have to fight Gilgamesh to gain his respect, but the woman wisely dissuades him. For

Text continued on page 144

Signature Seals: Treasures in Miniature

Cylinder seals—devices that impressed an individual's personal sign on documents and property—appeared in the Middle East 200 years before the invention of writing and remained in use for about 3,000 years. Made of stone, they were intricately carved with scenes of beasts and heroes, kings and gods; and they often doubled as amulets for their owners, for whom the seals represented a way of invoking the gods' good will.

To the modern historian, the seals provide a rich source for the study of Middle Eastern religion and mythology. With the advance of alphabetic Aramaic writing, cylinder seals—peculiarly adapted to imprinting the clay on which cuneiform was written—became obsolete; they gave way to stamp seals, which were better suited to leather and papyrus manuscripts.

A cylinder seal (above, left) was applied by rolling it across a surface of soft clay. The imprint of its design—a signature—is shown actual size (above, right), enlarged three times below.

On this 3,000-year-old seal, a supplicant approaches Ishtar, goddess of love. The tree and goats symbolize fertility and strength.

Gods and Heroes as Motifs

Mesopotamian cylinder seals changed with fashion and dealt with a great variety of popular myths. Heroes—mortal and earth-bound, yet endowed with super-human strength—prevail against ferocious beasts in the scenes below. Immortal gods conduct their eternal business with one another and with humans in the panels opposite. The inscriptions identify the seals' owners and often link them to the gods.

In a common mythical motif—pitting heroes and demigods against savage animals in a contest of strength—a hero wearing a head-dress of stylized curls struggles with two bulls (centre), while two long-haired figures fight rearing lions. The seal is about 4,500 years old.

A Sumerian hero thought to be Gilgamesh, fabled King of Uruk who was renowned for his encounters with beasts, wrestles a lion in two sequences separated by a decorative motif of plants. The seal dates from about 2260 B.C. and identifies its owner at right as the son of Abilum, a scribe.

143

In a seal from the First Millennium B.C., *the Sun God (centre) supports a solar disc; winged divinities keep watch as rain, suggesting growth, pours in symbolic streams from sky to earth. The inscription to the right of the Sun God names the seal's owner, Nabunasir, son of the priest of the god Adad.*

The mythical birdman Zu (centre) is hauled before the god of the sea (far right) by a minor goddess for trying to steal the tablet of destiny, inscribed with the fates of gods and men. Witnesses are a harvest deity carrying a plough (far left) and a god aiming a spear. The seal dates from 2200 B.C.

A bare-headed man—who could be Hashamer, a provincial governor in Sumer—is presented by his guardian goddess to the deified King of Ur, seated at right, while another deity follows at a respectful distance. The writing on the 4,000-year-old seal is a dedication by its owner to the King.

THE EARLIEST NOTATED MUSIC

The oldest piece of written music, a cult song in Hurrian cuneiform, was unearthed in the early 1950s at a Syrian dig near the ancient city of Ugarit. Deciphered in 1972, the four upper lines include lyrics containing the phrase "beloved of the heart" and references to gods and goddesses; the lower six contain instructions for performance—the equivalent of musical notation. The piece, written about 1800 B.C., establishes the Middle East as the birthplace of Western music.

Holding a replica of a 4,600-year-old lyre, musicologist Richard L. Crocker, of the University of California, Berkeley, prepares to play the Hurrian song. He was able to interpret the melody's pitches from the cuneiform but had to improvise the rhythm and tempo.

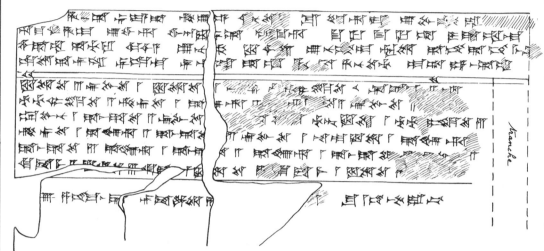

the night before the two arrive in Uruk, Gilgamesh has a dream and his wise mother interprets it to mean that a staunch new friend and comrade will presently appear before him. And so it turns out; Gilgamesh accepts the newly humanized Enkidu as a friend and counsellor, and together they wander through Sumer pursuing Gilgamesh's quest for immortality.

The story-tellers who composed this ancient morality tale were embroidering two of the deathless themes of literature: that there is a nobility in savage man; and that man and beast are kin, though the relationship may be all too easy to forget.

Another immortal theme, of course, is immortality itself—a subject carried to theatrical heights in the epic of Inanna, Sumerian queen of heaven, and her descent to the nether world. The oldest-known version was written during the first half of the Second Millennium B.C. on a number of cuneiform tablets found in Nippur. Only some 300 lines long, the Inanna story-poem is also descended from the old oral traditions. But written down, it has a special grace —suggesting a modern opera libretto so powerfully as to cry out for orchestra, proscenium and footlights. (The story may actually have been meant to be sung, at least in part; like many popular songs it has several repeated choruses and refrains. The work may even have been performed in a great hall, with a single voice singing the verses against a choir of many voices booming out the choruses.)

Inanna was also the goddess of love and fertility, and patroness of the city of Uruk. To the Babylonians she was later known as the love goddess Ishtar, and is also a prototype of the Greek Aphrodite and the Roman Venus. Under one such guise or another, she figured in a great many myths, but she decides in this poem, for reasons never adequately explained, to visit the nether world, which was ruled by her elder sister and bitter enemy. Ereshkigal, goddess of darkness and death. In the poem, adapted here from the translations of Sumerian scholar Samuel Noah

Kramer, Inanna prepares herself carefully for the journey ahead, first donning her most magnificent and costly finery and jewels:

> From the Great Above she set her mind towards
>   the Great Below.
> The *shugurra*, the crown of the plain, she put
>   upon her head,
> Radiance she placed upon her countenance,
> Sparkling stones she fastened to her breast,
> A gold ring she gripped in her hand,
> A breastplate she bound around her breast,
> All the garments of ladyship she put on her body.

But Inanna is aware of grave risks: the underworld is the Land of No Return—of death. So, as she sets out, she tells her faithful messenger, Ninshubur, that if she should not return within three days, he must appeal to three gods using the same words, beginning with Enlil, the chief god of the pantheon.

After these dramatic preparations, Inanna dismisses Ninshubur and descends to the underworld. When she reaches the jewelled palace there, she presents herself to Neti, the chief gatekeeper, and persuades him to report her arrival to her evil sister. The queen of the underworld agrees to let Inanna pass through its seven gates, but only in accordance with the established rules of her domain.

When Inanna reaches the first gate, her crown is removed from her head. She protests and is told:

> "Be silent, O Inanna, the decrees of the
>   nether world are perfect.
> O Inanna, do not question the rites of the
>   nether world."

At each of the seven gates this refrain is repeated, possibly by a choir. One by one Inanna's jewels and fine garments are removed from her, a process that appears to symbolize the shedding of worldly possessions at death. When Inanna passes the seventh gate, she presents herself naked at the court of Ereshkigal, who sits with the dreaded judges of the underworld. Together they "fasten their eyes upon her, the eyes of death". She is instantly turned into a corpse, and her body is hung from a stake.

At this point the story returns to the good messenger Ninshubur. As instructed, he has waited for three days and now fills heaven with complaints about the plight of his mistress Inanna. Dutifully he visits the temples of three gods, starting with the chief, and makes the appeal she has taught him:

> "Oh father Enlil, let not your daughter be put to death
>   in the nether world."

Three times, word for word, the faithful Ninshubur repeats the formula, and his efforts are finally successful. The third god to whom he appeals is Enki, the god of wisdom, who supplies the "water of life" and the "food of life" to be sprinkled 60 times on Inanna's corpse as it hangs on the stake. This done, the queen of heaven revives—in a denouement that is susceptible to several interpretations: it may be an allusion, ever popular among the ancients, to the rebirth of the earth in spring after winter's death; or it may be a simple affirmation that a goddess is not bound by the laws of mere mortals; or it may provide assurance that immortality is somehow always possible. In any event, Inanna ascends from the underworld accompanied by a retinue of large and small demons, who proceed to escort her to a noisy finale.

Indeed, *Inanna's Descent to the Nether World* has everything an opera needs; its main character confronts life's most fearsome fact—death—and is spared; as the goddess of love, she is the most beautiful woman in the world and she is gorgeously costumed. The story line calls for a sinister villain, her sister, and the action moves through an eventful journey—always good theatre; colourful settings —such as the jewelled palace—abound; the staging includes a lingering striptease, as Inanna is gradually denuded at the seven gates; and after the climactic confrontation, the heroine dies but lives again to figure in scores of other tales, wherein she plays rôles that signify all the baffling complexities and contradictions of love—constancy and fickleness, vengeance and mercy, jealousy and tenderness.

Such poetic narratives lay close to the core of life for most ancient Egyptians and Mesopotamians long before the Christian era. As they read and listened to these tales, they were obviously trying to penetrate the innumerable mysteries of the natural world to explain their own origins and past, to sort out the rights and wrongs of life and to cope with the fear of death. Though the barriers interposed by time are formidable, no thoughtful modern reader of the earliest literature can fail to recognize his kinship with its creators. And as archaeologists and linguists unearth and translate further samples of the oldest writing —gradually cleansing that historical windowpane of its ageless opacities and permitting a clearer, sharper view of the past—that consciousness of kinship must grow, thereby fulfilling, in a sense, mankind's perpetual dream of immortality.

Expressive Art of the Calligrapher

A poem is "a painting with a voice", according to the Japanese Zen masters. That view applies perhaps even more precisely to the art of writing as it was esteemed in ancient Japan, China and the world of Islam.

In Japan and China most accomplished painters and poets were primarily calligraphers; the tools they used—brush and ink—were the same for all three arts. True masters saw themselves raising the art of writing far beyond its purely utilitarian function of communication to a unique combination of literary and visual art. Often the meaning of a symbol was less important than the writer's mastery of visual form and style, the rhythm of his brushwork, the delicacy or boldness of his stroke.

In Islam, calligraphy was regarded as the highest of all art forms—a discipline for its own sake, an exercise in pure design. Islamic painters, discouraged by their faith from creating images of human beings, made the written word their means of recording beauty and paying homage to God. Muhammad's name or passages from the Koran—reversed, inverted and distorted—were worked into elaborate scrolls and arabesques. These calligraphic patterns, adapted by Muslim artisans in the decorations of rugs, pottery and buildings, were borrowed in turn by European craftsmen, who were impressed by the beauty of Islamic designs but ignorant of their origins. In the process, the Europeans created such anomalies as church doorways decorated with the Muslim confession of faith.

This exquisite calligraph, in a style known as slender gold, was the work of Hui-tsung, an emperor of China in the 12th century.

In the East, an Emphasis on Individual Style

To the greatest Chinese and Japanese calligraphers, the art of writing became a method of personal self-expression that went far beyond the meaning of written ideas. The finished work was intended to reflect not only the artist's individual perspective but even the emotional state in which he approached his assignment. Legibility became secondary; what counted was the writer's stylistic originality.

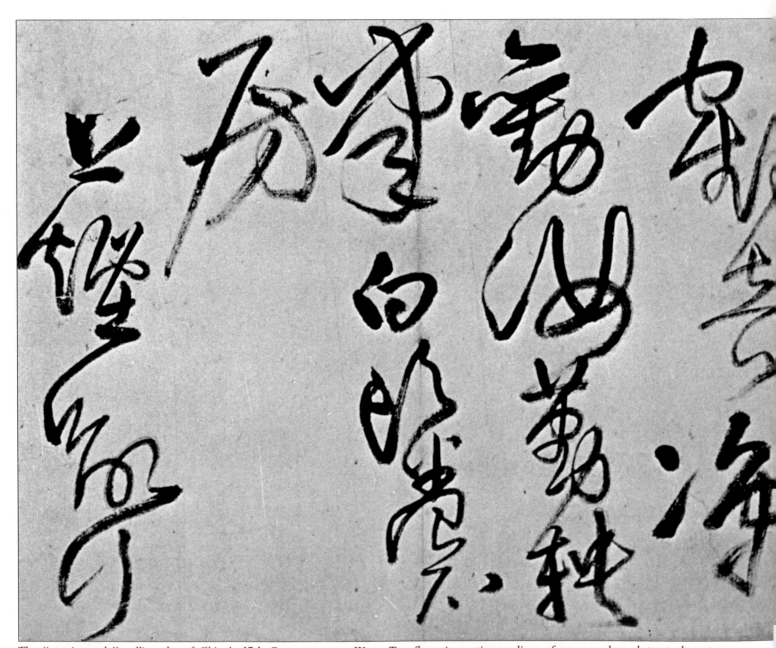

The "running-style" calligraphy of China's 17th Century master Wang Tuo flows in continuous lines of more or less abstract characters.

Poetry, painting and delicate free-form calligraphy are blended in two poems by Ikeno Taiga, Japan's 18th Century scholar-painter. The poems' subjects are suggested by ethereal illustrations —a black dog in the snow at right and a small boat and a riverbank at left.

This bold, even monumental, style of calligraphy was developed by one of Japan's great 18th Century Zen masters, Hakuin Ekaku. The words translate as "Blue-Countenanced-Bearer-of-the-Thunderbolt"—a Buddhist deity.

A Stately Script to Spread the Faith

Muslim scribes, who were the chief instrument in disseminating the word of the prophet Muhammad, delighted in ornamenting the sacred words of the Koran; they took special pride in the grace, balance and rhythm of their calligraphy. The intimate association of writing with the Islamic religion gave it lofty status, so much so that there was even a tradition that the *qualam*, or reed pen, was God's first creation.

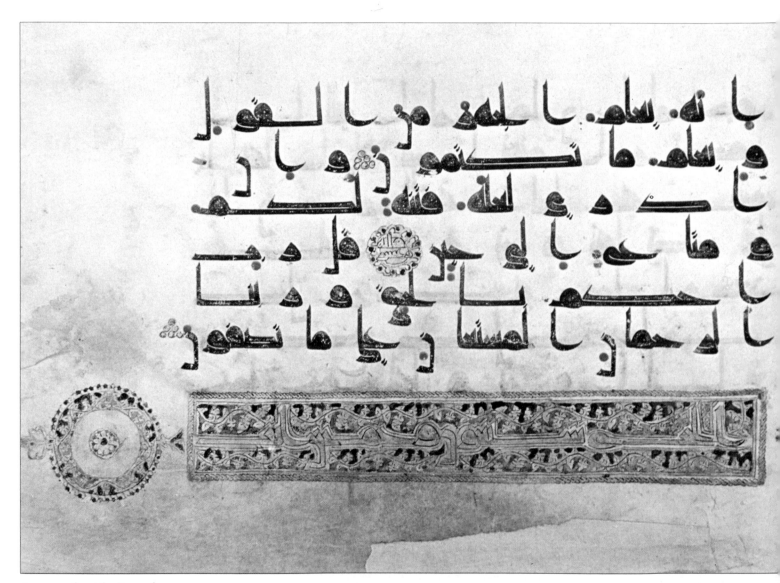

A passage from the Koran, by an unknown calligrapher, employs the classic Kufic script, so called after the city of Kufa, intellectual centre of Arabia in the ninth century. The style is still used today for ornate decoration in important official documents.

Set like a jewel within an elaborately embellished page of a 16th Century Persian Koran, this calligraphy is in the flowing Nastalik style. Students were taught to form their characters to evoke such features of birds as curving swans' necks and doves' wings.

Lettering to Enhance the Holy Word

Set off by exquisite borders and ornate initials, the opening pages of ninth-century Franco-Saxon sacred manuscripts were written in a clear style called uncial, a term derived from a Latin word meaning "one inch in size", though none of the letters were ever that large. Under Charlemagne's influence penmanship was standardized so that manuscripts became easier to read than earlier mediaeval writings.

A richly decorated letter Q and a page of uncial script begin the Gospel of Luke. Written in Latin, the manuscript was made by highly trained monks, probably at the Saint Armand Abbey in northern France. To create beautiful, uniform pages, scribes wrote in precise, rounded letters that enclosed large amounts of space.

Set inside a six-inch V, letters spelling the Latin word vere (truly) fill the opening page of a text produced in the ninth century.

The Emergence of Man

This chart records the progression of life on earth from its first appearance in the warm waters of the new-formed planet through the evolution of man himself; it traces his physical, social, technological and intellectual development to the Christian era. To place these advances in commonly used chronological sequences, the column at the

Geology	Archaeology	Thousand Millions of Years Ago	
Precambrian earliest era		4.5	Creation of the Earth
		4	Formation of the primordial sea
		3	First life, single-celled algae and bacteria, appears in water
		2	
		1	

		Millions of Years Ago	
			First oxygen-breathing animals appear
		800	
		600	Primitive organisms develop interdependent specialized cells
			Shell-bearing multicelled invertebrate animals appear
Palaeozoic ancient life			Evolution of armoured fish, first animals to possess backbones
		400	Small amphibians venture on to land
			Reptiles and insects arise
			Thecodont, ancestor of dinosaurs, arises
Mesozoic middle life		200	Age of dinosaurs begins
			Birds appear
			Mammals live in shadow of dinosaurs
			Age of dinosaurs ends
		80	
			Prosimians, earliest primates, develop in trees
Cainozoic recent life		60	
		40	Monkeys and apes evolve
		20	
		10	Ramapithecus, oldest known primate with apparently man-like traits, evolves in India and Africa
		8	
		6	
		4	Australopithecus, closest primate ancestor to man, appears in Africa

Geology	Archaeology	Millions of Years Ago	
Lower Pleistocene oldest period of most recent epoch	**Lower Palaeolithic** oldest period of Old Stone Age	2	Oldest known tool fashioned by man in Africa
		1	First true man, Homo erectus, emerges in East Indies and Africa
			Homo erectus populates temperate zones

		Thousands of Years Ago	
Middle Pleistocene middle period of most recent epoch		800	Man learns to control and use fire
		600	
		400	Large-scale, organized elephant hunts staged in Europe
			Man begins to make artificial shelters from branches
		200	
Upper Pleistocene latest period of most recent epoch	**Middle Palaeolithic** middle period of Old Stone Age		Neanderthal man emerges in Europe
		80	
		60	Ritual burials in Europe and Middle East suggest belief in afterlife
			Woolly mammoths hunted by Neanderthals in northern Europe
		40	Cave bear becomes focus of cult in Europe
	Upper Palaeolithic latest period of Old Stone Age		Cro-Magnon man arises in Europe
			Asian hunters cross Bering Land Bridge to populate New World
			Oldest known written record, lunar notations on bone, made in Europe
			Man reaches Australia
			First artists decorate walls and ceilings of caves in France and Spain
		30	Figurines sculpted for nature worship
		20	Invention of needle makes sewing possible
			Bison hunting begins on Great Plains of North America
Holocene present epoch	**Mesolithic** Middle Stone Age	10	Bow and arrow invented in Europe
			Pottery first made in Japan

(Last Ice Age — spanning Upper Pleistocene through to Holocene)

▼ Four thousand million years ago   ▼ Three thousand million years ago

▲ Origin of the Earth (4,500 million)   ▲ First life (3,500 million)

left of each of the chart's four sections identifies the great geo-
logical eras into which the earth's history is divided by scientists,
while the second column lists the archaeological ages of human history. The key dates in the rise of life and of man's outstanding
accomplishments appear in the third column (years and events men-

tioned in this volume of The Emergence of Man appear in bold type).
The chart is not to scale; the reason is made clear by the bar below,
which represents in linear scale the 4,500 million years spanned by the
chart—on the scaled bar, the portion relating to the total period of
known human existence (*far right*) is too small to be distinguished.

Geology	Archaeology	Years B.C.	
Holocene *(cont.)*	Neolithic New Stone Age	9000	
			Sheep domesticated in Middle East
			Dog domesticated in North America
		8000	Jericho, oldest known city, settled
			Goat domesticated in Persia
			Man cultivates his first crops, wheat and barley, in Middle East
		7000	Pattern of village life grows in Middle East
			Catal Hüyük, in what is now Turkey, becomes largest Neolithic city
			Loom invented in Middle East
			Cattle domesticated in Middle East
	Copper Age	6000	Agriculture begins to replace hunting in Europe
			Copper used in trade in Mediterranean area
			Corn cultivated in Mexico
		4800	Oldest known massive stone monument built in Brittany
		4000	Sail-propelled boats used in Egypt
			First city-states develop in Sumer
			Cylinder seals begin to be used as marks of identification in Middle East
		3500	First potatoes grown in South America
			Wheel originates in Sumer
			Man begins to cultivate rice in Far East
			Silk moth domesticated in China
			Horse domesticated in south Russia
			Egyptian merchant trading ships start to ply the Mediterranean
			Pictograph writing invented in Middle East
	Bronze Age	3000	Bronze first used to make tools in Middle East
			City life spreads to Nile Valley
			Plough is developed in Middle East
			Accurate calendar based on stellar observation devised in Egypt
		2800	Stonehenge, most famous of ancient stone monuments, begun in England
			Pyramids built in Egypt
			Minoan navigators begin to venture into seas beyond the Mediterranean

Geology	Archaeology	Years B.C.	
Holocene *(cont.)*	Bronze Age *(cont.)*	2600	**Variety of gods and heroes glorified in *Gilgamesh* and other epics in Middle East**
		2500	Cities rise in the Indus Valley
			Earliest evidence of use of skis in Scandinavia
			Earliest written code of laws drawn up in Sumer
		2000	Use of bronze in Europe
			Chicken and elephant domesticated in Indus Valley
			Eskimo culture begins in Bering Strait area
		1500	Invention of ocean-going outrigger canoes enables man to reach islands of South Pacific
			Ceremonial bronze sculptures created in China
			Imperial government, ruling distant provinces, established by Hittites
		1400	Iron in use in Middle East
			First complete alphabet devised in script of the Ugarit people in Syria
			Hebrews introduce concept of monotheism
	Iron Age	1000	Reindeer domesticated in Eurasia
			Phoenicians spread alphabet
		900	
		800	Use of iron begins to spread throughout Europe
			First highway system built in Assyria
			Homer composes *Iliad* and *Odyssey*
			Mounted nomads appear in the Middle East as a new and powerful force
		700	Rome founded
			Wheel barrow invented in China
		200	Epics about India's gods and heroes, the *Mahabharata* and *Ramayana*, written
			Water wheel invented in Middle East
		0	Christian era begins

▼ Two thousand million years ago   ▼ One thousand million years ago

First oxygen-breathing animals (900 million) ▲   First animals to possess backbones (470 million) ▲   First men (1.3 million) ▲

Credits

The sources for the illustrations in this book are shown below. Credits from left to right are separated by semicolons, from top to bottom by dashes.

Cover—Painting by Ron Lesser. 8—British Museum, London. 10—Ashmolean Museum, Oxford. 12—Paulus Leeser courtesy Economic & Public Affairs Division, The New York Public Library, Astor, Lenox and Tilden Foundations—The Historical Society of Pennsylvania. 13—Paulus Leeser courtesy Economic & Public Affairs Division, The New York Public Library, Astor, Lenox and Tilden Foundations. 14—Collection Musée de l'Homme, Paris. 17—Courtesy National Museum of Victoria Council, except bottom right, Radio Times Hulton Picture Library. 18—Courtesy of The American Museum of Natural History. 23 to 31—Paulus Leeser courtesy Oriental Division, The New York Public Library, Astor, Lenox and Tilden Foundations. 32—Giraudon courtesy Musée du Louvre, Paris. 35—Hirmer Fotoarchiv courtesy Egyptian Museum, Cairo. 36—The Bettmann Archive. 37—Eno Collection, Prints Division, The New York Public Library, Astor, Lenox and Tilden Foundations—The Bettmann Archive. 40—British Museum, London. 41—Roger Viollet—Paulus Leeser courtesy Oriental Division, The New York Public Library, Astor, Lenox and Tilden Foundations; Heinz Zinram courtesy British Museum, London. 44, 45—Brian Brake from Rapho Guillumette. 48—Manuscript from Ottobonian Latin Archives, Vatican Library—British Museum, London. 51—Archiv für Kunst und Geschichte, Berlin. 53—Royal Danish Library, Copenhagen. 54, 55—Paulus Leeser courtesy Oriental Division, The New York Public Library, Astor, Lenox and Tilden Foundations, except bottom left, Oriental Division, The New York Public Library, Astor, Lenox and Tilden Foundations. 56, 57—Thames & Hudson, Ltd., London—General Research & Humanities Division, The New York Public Library, Astor, Lenox and Tilden Foundations; Paulus Leeser courtesy Oriental Division, The New York Public Library,

brary, Astor, Lenox and Tilden Foundations. 58, 59—Paulus Leeser courtesy Oriental Division, The New York Public Library, Astor, Lenox and Tilden Foundations. 60—Réunion des Musées Nationaux. 64, 65—Dr. Georg Gerster from Rapho Guillumette. 66—Courtesy of The Oriental Institute, University of Chicago. 67—(Left) The Walters Art Gallery, Baltimore; (Centre) University Museum, University of Pennsylvania; (Right) British Museum, London. 69—Courtesy of The Oriental Institute, University of Chicago. 71—Pierre Boulat courtesy Musée du Louvre, Paris. 72—Al-Hiba Expedition of The Metropolitan Museum of Art and The Institute of Fine Arts, New York; Maurice Chuzeville courtesy Musée du Louvre, Paris. 73—Luc Joubert courtesy Archaeological Museum, Tehran. 74—University Museum, University of Pennsylvania. 77—Courtesy of The Oriental Institute, University of Chicago, except top left, University Museum, University of Pennsylvania. 79 to 85—Drawings by Don Bolognese. 86—Brian Brake from Rapho Guillumette. 89—University Museum, University of Pennsylvania—Courtesy of The Oriental Institute, University of Chicago. 90—British Museum, London. 93—Courtesy of The Oriental Institute, University of Chicago; Brian Brake from Rapho Guillumette courtesy Egyptian Museum, Cairo. 94—Brian Brake from Rapho Guillumette. 95—Brian Brake from Rapho Guillumette courtesy British Museum, London. 96—Robert Colton courtesy The Brooklyn Museum; F. L. Kenett, photo copyright George Rainbird Ltd.; Maurice Chuzeville courtesy Musée du Louvre, Paris. 98, 99—Brian Brake from Rapho Guillumette courtesy Egyptian Museum, Cairo. 102—Paulus Leeser courtesy Science & Technology Research Center, The New York Public Library, Astor, Lenox and Tilden Foundations; Robert Colton courtesy The Brooklyn Museum. 103—Robert Colton courtesy The Brooklyn Museum. 105—Courtesy Egyptian Museum, Cairo. 107—F. L. Kenett, photo copyright George Rainbird Ltd. 108—The Metropolitan Museum of Art, Rogers Fund, 1917; The Metropolitan Museum of Art, Gifts from Various Donors, 1926. 109—The Metropolitan Museum of Art,

Gift of Edward S. Harkness, 1926. 110, 111—Brian Brake from Rapho Guillumette. 112, 113—Brian Brake from Rapho Guillumette. 114—Larry Burrows, TIME-LIFE Picture Agency, © 1972 Time Incorporated. 116—Lynn St. John, TIME-LIFE Picture Agency, © 1972 Time Incorporated. 119—Professor Willard G. Oxtoby. 121—Map by Rafael D. Palacios. 122—Gabinetto Fotografico Nazionale courtesy Museo Pigorini, Rome—Deutsches Archäologisches Institut, Athens; M. A. Kislali courtesy Archaeological Museum of Istanbul. 123—Hirmer Fotoarchiv, Munich courtesy Musée du Louvre, Paris—Archives Photographiques courtesy Musée du Louvre, Paris. 127—Annivas Stamatopoulos courtesy The Heraklion Museum, Crete—Aldo Durazzi. 128—Larry Burrows, TIME-LIFE Picture Agency, © 1972 Time Incorporated; Emmett Bright courtesy National Museum of Pakistan, Karachi. 129—Emmett Bright courtesy National Museum of Pakistan, Karachi. 130—Dmitri Kessel, TIME-LIFE Picture Agency, © 1972 Time Incorporated. 131—Paulus Leeser from J. Eric S. Thompson, *A Commentary on the Dresden Codex*, MEMOIRS of the American Philosophical Society, Vol. 93 (1972). 132—Fotocielo. 133—Aldo Durazzi courtesy Soprintendenza alle Antichita' dell' Etruria Meridionale, Rome. 134—Larry Burrows, TIME-LIFE Picture Agency, © 1972 Time Incorporated—Photograph by Alison Frantz courtesy University of Cincinnati. 135—Tom Blau from Camera Press. 136—Réunion des Musées Nationaux. 139—Maurice Chuzeville courtesy Musée du Louvre, Paris. 141, 142, 143—Werner Forman Archive. 144—Copyright Professor Claude Schaeffer; Photograph by Dennis Galloway for University of California, Berkeley. 147—National Palace Museum, Taipei. 148—National Palace Museum, Taipei. 149—Photograph by Konishi Biendo courtesy Kiyoo Yamamoto; Frank Lerner courtesy Philadelphia Museum of Art. 150, 151—Continental Oil Company, 1974 Islamic Calendar courtesy The Turkish Islamic Arts Museum, Suleyman Mosque, Istanbul. 152, 153—Courtesy The Pierpont Morgan Library.

Acknowledgments

For the help given in the preparation of this book, the editors are particularly indebted to Baruch A. Levine, Chairman, Department of Near Eastern Languages and Literature, New York University, and Richard Fazzini, Assistant Curator, Department of Egyptian and Classical Art, Brooklyn Museum, New York City. The editors also express their gratitude to Pentti Aalto, Professor of Comparative Philology, University of Helsinki, Finland; Mrs. Sule Aksoy, Section Chief, Museum of Turkish and Islamic Art, Istanbul, Turkey; Pierre Amiet, Chief Curator, Department of Oriental Antiquities, Louvre Museum, Paris; Paul Barguet, Director, Institute of Egyptology, University of Lyons, France; Catherine Bélanger, Louvre Museum, Paris; the Reverend Charles Burns, Vatican Library, Rome; Silvio Curto, Superintendent, Egyptian Antiquities, Turin, Italy; George F. Dales, Professor of South Asian and Near Eastern Archeology, University of California at Berkeley; David Diringer, Director, Alphabet Museum, Tel Aviv; I. E. S. Edwards, Department of Egyptian Antiquities, British Museum, London; Felice Fisher,

Assistant Curator of Far Eastern Art, Philadelphia Museum of Art, Pennsylvania; Ali Hakemi, Professor of Archaeology and director of excavation unit, Shahdad, Iran; Diane Harlé, Department of Egyptian Antiquities, Louvre Museum, Paris; Max Hirmer, formerly professor at Munich University, Germany; Herbert Kessler, Chairman, Department of Art, University of Chicago; Nikolaos Kontoleon, Inspector General of the Archaeological Services of Greece; Jean Gordon Lee, Curator of Far Eastern Art, Philadelphia Museum of Art, Pennsylvania; Guglielmo Maetzke, Superintendent, Etruscan Antiquities, Florence, Italy; T. C. Mitchell, Department of Western Asiatic Antiquities, British Museum, London; J. Papapostolou, Director, Crania Museum, Crete; Asko Heikki Siegfried Parpola, Associate Professor of Indology, University of Helsinki, Finland; André Parrot, French Institute, Paris; Tatiana Proskouriakoff, Peabody Museum, Harvard University, Cambridge, Massachusetts; Issa Salman, Director, and Fawzi Rashid, Iraq Museum, Baghdad; C. F. A. Schaeffer, French Institute, Paris; Abdul-Hussein Shahidzadeh, Archaeological Museum of Iran, Tehran; A. F. Shore, Department of Egyptian Antiquities, British Museum, London; Françoise Tallon, Researcher, Department of Oriental Antiquities, Louvre Museum, Paris; Maurizio Tosi, Italian Institute of Middle and Far Eastern Studies, Rome; Pierre Vaillant, Chief Curator, Principal Library, Grenoble, France; A. L. West, Curator, Department of Anthropology, National Museum of Victoria, Australia.

Bibliography

Archaeology

Aldred, Cyril, *Egypt to the End of the Old Kingdom* (Library of Early Civilizations). Thames and Hudson, 1965.

Braidwood, Robert J., and Gordon R. Willey, eds., *Courses Toward Urban Life*. Edinburgh University Press.

Ceram, C. W., *Gods, Graves and Scholars*. Gollancz, 1971.

*Ehrich, Robert W., ed., *Chronologies in Old World Archaeology*. University of Chicago Press, 1965.

*Greener, Leslie, *The Discovery of Egypt*. The Viking Press, 1966.

*Hansen, Thorkild, *Arabia Felix*. Translated from the Danish by James and Kathleen McFarlane. Harper and Row, 1964.

Jidejian, Nina, *Byblos Through the Ages*. Argonaut Inc., 1969.

Mallowan, M. E. L., *Early Mesopotamia and Iran* (Library of Early Civilizations). Thames and Hudson, 1965.

Marshack, Alexander, *The Roots of Civilization*. Weidenfeld and Nicolson, 1972.

*Moscati, Sabatino, *The Face of the Ancient Orient*. Doubleday, 1962.

Decipherment

Chadwick, John, *The Decipherment of Linear*. Cambridge University Press, 1968.

Cottrell, Leonard, *Reading the Past*, J. M. Dent, 1972.

*Doblhofer, Ernst, *Voices in Stone*. Translated from the German by Mervyn Savill. The Viking Press, 1961.

Gordon, Cyrus H., *Forgotten Scripts*. Thames and Hudson, 1968; Penguin Books, 1971.

History

Beek, Martin A., *Atlas of Mesopotamia*. Translated from the Dutch by D. R. Welsh. Thomas Nelson and Sons, 1962

Bottero, Jean, Elean Cassin and Jean Vercoutter, eds., *The Near East: The Early Civilizations*. Translated from the French by R. F. Tannenbaum, Weidenfeld and Nicolson, 1968.

Drower, Margaret S., *Ugarit*. Cambridge University Press, 1968.

Edwards, I. E. S., C. J. Chadd and N. G. L. Hammond, eds., *The Cambridge Ancient History*. 3rd ed., Vol. 1, Part 2. Cambridge University Press, 1971.

Frye, Richard N., *The Heritage of Persia*. Weidenfeld and Nicolson, 1963.

*Cahill, James, *Scholar Painters of Japan; The Nanga School*. The Asian Society Inc., 1972.

*Chiang, Yee, *Chinese Calligraphy: An Introduction to its Aesthetic and Technique*. Harvard University Press, 1973.

*Chiera, Edward, *They Wrote on Clay*. University of Chicago Press, 1966.

Cleator, P. E., *Lost Languages*. Robert Hale and Company, 1973.

*Clodd, Edward, *The Story of the Alphabet*. (Facsimile reprint of the 1938 edition by D. Appleton Century Co. Inc.). Gale Research Co., 1970.

*Day, Cyrus Lawrence, *Quipus and Witches' Knots*. University of Kansas Press, 1967.

Diringer, David:
  The Alphabet. 2 vols. Hutchinson, 1968.
  Writing (Ancient Peoples and Places). Thames and Hudson, 1962.

Friedrich, Johannes, *Extinct Languages*. Peter Owen, 1962.

Gardiner, Sir Alan, *Egyptian Grammar*. Oxford University Press, 1957.

Gelb, I. J. A., *A Study of Writing*. University of Chicago Press, 1952.

*Jones, Tom B., ed., *The Sumerian Problem*. John Wiley and Sons, Inc., 1969.

*Lee, James Zee-min, *Chinese Potpourri*. The Oriental Press, 1950.

Mallery, Garrick, *Picture-writing of the American Indians*. Dover Publications, 1973.

Pei, Mario, *The Story of Language*. Allen and Unwin, 1968.

*Rosenfeld, John M., Fumiko, E., and Edwin A. Cranston, *The Courtly Tradition in Japanese Art and Literature*. Fogg Art Museum, Harvard University, 1973.

*Scott, Joseph and Lenore, *Egyptian Hieroglyphics for Everyone*. Funk and Wagnalls, 1968.

Tsien, Tsuen-hsuin, *Written on Bamboo and Silk*. University of Chicago Press, 1962.

Wilson, John, *Signs and Wonders upon Pharaoh*. University of Chicago Press, 1964.

*Wiseman, D. J., ed., *Cylinder Seals of Western Asia*. Batchworth Press, n.d.

*Yamagiwa, Joseph K., *Introduction to Japanese Writing*. George Wahr Publishing Co., 1966.

*Jastrow, Morris, Jr., *The Civilization of Babylonia and Assyria*. J. B. Lippincott, Co., 1915.

Kramer, Samuel Noah, *The Sumerians*. University of Chicago Press, 1963.

Oppenheim, A. Leo, *Ancient Mesopotamia: Portrait of a Dead Civilization*. University of Chicago Press, 1970.

*Pritchard, James B., ed., *The Ancient Near East in Pictures*. Princeton University Press, 1969.

Roux, Georges, *Ancient Iraq*. Allen and Unwin, 1964; Penguin Books, 1969.

Saggs, H. W. F., *The Greatness that was Babylon*. Sidgwick and Jackson, 1962.

Vervliet, H. D. L., ed., *The Book Through 5000 Years*. Phaidon Press, 1972.

Wilson, John A., *The Culture of Ancient Egypt*. University of Chicago Press, 1956.

Wiseman, D. J., ed., *Peoples of Old Testament Times*. Oxford University Press, 1973.

Woolley, Sir Leonard, and Jacquetta Hawkes, *Prehistory and the Beginnings of Civilization*. Allen and Unwin, 1963.

Translations

*Erman, Adolf, *The Literature of the Ancient Egyptians*. Translated from the German by Aylward M. Blackman. Benjamin Blom Inc., reissued, 1971.

*Faulkner, R. O., Edward F. Wente Jr., and William Kelly Simpson, translators, *The Literature of Ancient Egypt: An Anthology of Stories, Instructions and Poetry*. Yale University Press, 1972.

*Grayson, A. K., and Donald B. Redford, eds., *Papyrus and Tablet*. Prentice-Hall, Inc., 1973.

*Kramer, Samuel Noah, *History Begins at Sumer*. Doubleday, 1959.

Oppenheim, A. Leo, *Letters from Mesopotamia*. University of Chicago Press, 1967.

Pritchard, James B., ed., *Ancient Near Eastern Texts Relating to the Old Testament*. Princeton University Press, 1970.

Wente, Edward F., *Late Ramesside Letters*. University of Chicago Press, 1967.

Writing and Calligraphy

Anderson, Donald M., *The Art of Written Forms*. Holt, Rinehart and Winston, Inc., 1969.

* *Art of Writing*. United Nations Educational.

*Published in the U.S. only.

Index

Numerals in italics indicate an illustration of the subject mentioned.

Filmsetting by C. E. Dawkins (Typesetters) Ltd., London, SE1 1UN
Printed and bound in Belgium by Brepols Fabrieken N.V.